Oregon's Salty Coast

The Oregon Coast at a Glance

ESTUARIES
1. Columbia River
2. Nehalem River
3. Tillamook Bay
4. Netarts Bay
5. Nestucca River
6. Salmon River
7. Siletz River
8. Yaquina River
9. Alsea River
10. Siuslaw River
11. Umpqua River
12. Coos Bay
13. Coquille River
14. Rogue River
15. Chetco River

HEADLANDS
16. Tillamook Head
17. Cape Falcon
18. Cape Meares
19. Cape Lookout
20. Cape Kiwanda
21. Cascade Head
22. Cape Foulweather
    (Otter Crest)
23. Yaquina Head
24. Cape Perpetua
25. Heceta Head
26. Cape Arago
27. Cape Blanco
28. Cape Sebastian
29. Cape Ferrelo

BEACHES
30. Clatsop Beach
31. Cannon Beach
32. Beverly Beach
33. Agate Beach
34. Bastendorff Beach

COVES
35. Boiler Bay
36. Whale Cove
37. Depoe Bay
38. Sand Lake
39. Sunset Bay
40. Hunters Cove

OFFSHORE ROCKS & REEFS
41. Haystack Rock
    (Cannon Beach)
42. Haystack Rock
    (Pacific City)
43. Stonewall Bank
44. Heceta Bank
45. Rogue River Reef
46. Orford Reef
47. Mack Arch

OTHER LANDMARKS
48. Sea Lion Caves
49. Sand dune area
50. Neahkahnie Mountain
51. Humbug Mountain

ASTORIA
SEASIDE
TILLAMOOK
PACIFIC CITY
LINCOLN CITY
DEPOE BAY
NEWPORT
WALDPORT
YACHATS
FLORENCE
REEDSPORT
COOS BAY
BANDON
PORT ORFORD
GOLD BEACH
BROOKINGS

Oregon's Salty Coast

From Explorers to the Present Time

James A. "Jim" Gibbs
With Bert Webber

Webb Research Group Publishers
Books About the Oregon Country

Cover picture:
"Children at the Beach"
Pacific City, Oregon
by Rosalie Webber
35mm Fujicolor ASA200
Olympus iS-1 Zoom 35-135mm

Address all inquiries to the Publisher:
WEBB RESEARCH GROUP
P.O. Box 314
Medford, OR 97501 U.S.A.

Library of Congress Cataloging in Publication Data

Gibbs, Jim, 1922
    Oregon's salty coast / James A. "Jim" Gibbs : with Bert
Webber.
      p.   cm.
    Includes bibliographical references and index.
    ISBN 0-936738-82-0
    1. Pacific Coast (Or.)–History. I. Webber, Bert. II. Title
F882.P34G53   1994   94-9939
979.6–dc20   CIP

Contents

OREGON COAST
PRETTY·AS·A·PICTURE

Arizona Beach on the Curry County coast.

Oregon Coast — Pretty as a Picture

Of over 200 photographs the editors reviewed for possible use in this book, they selected some as best meeting these guide lines:

Must be an Oregon Coast scene.
Must be a subject that can be seen by visitors.
Picture must excite viewers at first glance.
The photograph must meet the general standards of artistic composition.
Camera and darkroom work must be "straight" – no tricks.

The photographs are found on these pages:

Cover, vi, vii, **19, 22, 23, 30, 35, 95, 136, 137, 138, 140, 156, 157, 164, 165, 168**

This was not a contest. There were no prizes however the photographers, some who requested not to be listed by name, each received a gift copy of this book. Those who agreed to the use of their names are on the Illustration Credits page 171.

←**Yaquina Head lighthouse is near Newport.**

Hug Point, on the north Oregon coast, is historically important
because this shelf-like roadway was carved out of solid rock to
permit vehicles to pass the point during high tide. Otherwise,
horse-drawn wagons, as well as early automobiles, stayed on
the wet, sandy beach.

Introduction

For those whose ears are so attuned there comes a call from the seashore down Oregon way. For precisely 363 miles, not counting coastal indentations, this salty frontier meets either in harmonious nature or vicious combat. Fantastic seascapes, iridescent tide pools, wet glistening sands and white-lipped breakers are sights once seen, never forgotten. The undeniable forces of nature sometimes create titanic storm waves that crash against bold, rocky headlands urged on by howling winter winds that uproot giant trees above the coastline. Worn down sea stacks standing sentinel bear scars of massive erosion from the persistence of the unrelenting combers. There are always the little marine creatures scrambling for a place to hide until the onslaught has subsided. Wet, penetrating fogs often drop their mantles as if on cat's paws. Sometimes the world seems completely closed down under a misty veil.

Man stands virtually helpless when voluminous liquid battering rams pound against Oregon's formidable shores whittling away morsels of terra firma. In this hostile battleground where the land meets the sea, the latter has consistently been the victor and will continue to be until the end of the age. As Oregon slowly shrinks, the mighty Pacific expands.

Ah, the Pacific! Often peaceful, sometimes violent, an unpredictable personality so akin to a woman, and subject to change without notice.

Life in and around Oregon's Pacific rim is always fascinating, past or present. Here, the sea has a heartbeat far more enduring and infinite than that of man. The pulse of the tidal flow, the breath of the full gale or the whisper of the surf are all messages to delight the senses. Yes, here, even the seashell from its hollow innards has a story to tell. Awesome, placid or terri-

High surf is photogenic on the Oregon coast especially during winter storms. At Seaside (top) a breaker crashes on the seawall. For another view of this beach see page 143. (Lower) Margie Webber dashes back from the edge of rip-rap north of Nesika Beach.

fying, this fantastic ocean front has a magnetic power. Watching a great golden orb drown itself in the western sea at day's end or following the rippling silver path of the moon's reflection can virtually cause an hypnotic spell.

Those who work the coastal waters gain a respectful fear when great liquid acclivity's rise and unceremoniously toss about the largest of floating conveyances. Solomon knew the feeling so long ago when he declared: "One of the great wonders is the way of a ship on the sea." Nor is the puniness of man ever more obvious than when his craft lies mangled on a hostile outcrop or plunges to its doom in irascible waters.

There exists an indissoluble trinity, other than that of the spiritual, between the sea, the ship and man. At times they love and reverence each other and on other occasions breed the most hostile contempt, but always there is reconciliation. Men and ships are dependent on each other but the ocean has been described as a mother, a mistress and a temptress.

The human element that plays its part in this continuing drama – master mariner, common sailor, artist, writer, fisherman, clam digger, rockhound or beachcomber – each has formed a deep-rooted awe and respect of Oregon's offshore waters and its coastal ramparts. Many immortals with the pen, many geniuses with the brush, and others through the spoken word have added enduring flavor to this amazing coastline. Symphonies composed by man have limitations but the symphony of the sea is virtually eternal with auras unlimited. Nor has any author, no matter how talented, ever fully captured the personality of the sea, nor artist its complete beauty.

The thought is ever present that the sea goes on and on long after ships vanish and man is reduced to ashes. And though God promised never again to flood the earth, the ocean still occupies the greater proportion of our sphere and each year accumulates more and more land for conversion into the watery kingdom.

In modern years with his ever-increasing technology, man has attempted to bridge the seas with ever larger vessels some longer than five football fields. He has further attempted to control the undersea world with scientific submarines but more so with the highly feared nuclear-powered submersibles armed with death-dealing missiles equipped with nuclear warheads waiting the signal for genocide action.

The goal is no longer discovery, but control. Then there is the dread of man wantonly destroying the sea, his greatest asset, through pollution. But, polluted or not, the ocean will continue to roll against a thousand shores, not the least of which is Oregon, where the Pacific, the world's greatest water source, puts on its finest show.

Since the initial stirrings of human imagination, the sea and the shore have enthralled. From the dawn of literature, man has chronicled his nautical wanderings. When man has a story to tell he will tell it in the best way he knows be it by petroglyph or pen, and the world is richer for his efforts. Men have written of the sea and shore since 2500 B.C., when an unknown author set down on papyrus an account of his battle with a sea serpent, a document preserved in the British Museum.

The real beginning, however, goes back in the eons of time when God created the heavens and the earth, where Genesis reads:

> God said, let there be a firmament in the midst of the waters, and let it divide the waters from the waters. And God made the firmament and divided the waters which were under the firmament from the waters which were above the firmament: and it was so. And God said; Let the waters under the heaven be gathered together unto one place and let the dry land appear: and it was so. And God called the dry land Earth; and the gathering together of the waters called he Seas: and God saw that it was good.

Oregon was formed amidst a great terrestrial revolution with vast eruptions of lava. The earth quaked violently valleys being deeply notched and mountains formed. Long rollers broke on the coasts of a hot earth. After the creation it awaited mortal man, but man who permitted sin to creep in caused God to repent of his works and the world was inundated. The cataclysmic wonder that would one day be known as Oregon was submerged.

From Noah's Ark down to our day some unknown ingredient has continued to pull man to the seashore and to the ocean. Ironically, that elemental, ageless tow remains as strong in the nuclear age as it did in antiquity. In essence, all of us are islanders, inhabitants of the only water planet known to man in the solar system. The seas of our globe surround all the continents making them islands in one massive ocean. Fishes live in a domain much deeper than the land's highest mountain, and more than a third larger in size than all the land mass combined.

The sea even breeds the weather and dominates the climate. The seafarer, on seeing a storm building only has two alternatives: He can either run for safe haven ashore or ride it out. The safe havens are relatively few and far between along the Oregon coast and rough bar entrances in adverse conditions will neither permit marine traffic to enter nor to depart. Melville said that the sea "will insult and murder man and pulverize his most rugged ships." Conrad focuses on its unfathomable cruelty. Still, its good far outweighs its bad. Even the best of humans has an occasional display of temper.

In ancient times, the sea was looked upon with a fearful eye, a treacherous place to be avoided by sane men. To get out of

> **The first commandment for the Oregon beachcomber is to never turn his back on the ocean. When the ocean's mood is angry beware! Many have failed to heed the rule and many have not lived to tell the tale.**

sight of land was not only considered foolhardy, but downright suicidal. Today the oceans are explored and charted in every corner and modem communications keep them down to size. Still, it has an aura of incomparable excitement and attraction. The ocean's unbridled fury is responsible each year for a heavy toll in lives and property but that certain scintillating and intriguing ingredient coupled with mystery and surprise will never cease as long as man breathes fresh sea air.

No place on this earth, we repeat, does the ocean put on a better show than along the Oregon coast. The Continental Shelf has a gentle slope westward to the deep troughs well offshore. On gentle days, the combers spill over like miniature waterfalls, and again, when the northerly and southerly winds blast, or a storm has occurred far out at sea, the surf becomes a mass of confused white water boiling and hissing like a witch's brew. When giant breakers lash the stern, rock-bound sectors, geysers often soar skyward or shoot jet streams into the air through blowholes. Deep fissures formed by the constant pounding through countless centuries are continually eroded by seas that end their long journeys by snubbing their noses against the solid basalt of the Oregon coast. Walls of brine pulverize the softer earth above creating further wearing and incurable scars. Sometimes the surf is stirred into a frenzied froth like the residue from tens of thousands of washing machines bathing the shoreline in a foamy mass deadening the sound of the shore breakers.

The ocean in motion is probably the most constant and dependable show on earth. We marvel at the human heart and its perpetual beat from birth to death, but consider the pulse of the ocean that has been going on in a continuing action since well before man. In a constant state of upheaval, waves, tidal action and currents team up along the shoreline to disperse the sediment that comes down from the hinterland via the many Oregon rivers and streams. In the upheaval, millions of tons of sand are shifted around constantly supplying the numerous beaches which are

13

The north Oregon coast is relatively rock-free, however in the south the geology is completely different.

divided from the more defiant rocky sections. Outcrops by the score have been cut off from the mainline of resistance standing like brave soldiers fighting a helpless cause, rotund, flat, slanted and craggy shapes, fending off the watery fusillades.

To the oceanographers and scientists, we leave the technical side of the marine, but it's a comforting thought to know that God made it so that the more simple-minded can enjoy the pranks of the ocean and its shoreline every bit as much, if not more so than those who make it a profession. It doesn't take much training to learn that the tides run their course two times a day clockwise, beginning around an axis out in mid-ocean affected in their mysterious ways by the pull of the moon, the effect of the sun and of the earth itself. The cycle affords two highs and two lows and the places where the ranges are the greatest afford the grandest probing grounds for the beachcomber and vacationer.

Some of the unusual seashore creatures endure the dry spells until covered by the incoming tides while others scramble for the water when their habitats become landlocked, nestle down deep in the sand or hold out on their rocky perches. The moon, some 239,000 miles out in space, unaffected by the junk left by our spacemen, continues its undeniable pull at the surface of our earth. Though rocks are immovable, the ocean responds to the pull, and as oceanographers say, humps up liquidly. On the other side of the world, a similar situation takes place due to the opposing centrifugal force of the earth curving in its orbit, which in a way of speaking almost matches the pull of the moon.

Way, way out in space, some 93 million miles, ol' Sol exerts its slight but definite influence with a pull reinforcing the effect of the moon when the two bodies are aligned. The moon, which appears to be of little use to our traditional way of life, is in actuality a vital part of our existence and should it ever be blasted out of space could have a deadly effect on our world. Its irregular orbit around planet earth causes the extreme tides when it comes the closest. Man should remember this when he enjoys the fascination of the minus tides or watches the watery onslaught of the flood tides inundating acres of previously attainable shore lands.

Though many maritime areas such as Hawaii and the South

Winter storms remove then heave driftwood on nearly every tide.

Pacific, due to their geographical locations, are deprived of extreme tidal fluctuations, the Oregon shoreline enjoys a veritable housecleaning with each change of tide. The extreme fluctuations running from an extreme high of plus ten to a minus three feet. Beachcombers love the high tides because of the treasures King Neptune leaves on the sand. And the diggers, armed with "clam guns" plan their trips to the beach on the minus tide days. Of course, when storm waves accompany high tides, the inundated area will increase appreciably though it does not compare to Canada's Bay of Fundy with the greatest tidal fluctuations in the world. That inlet of the Atlantic has tides or bore to 70 feet, and many of its flatlands have been diked off and reclaimed

Some of the gradual slopes along Oregon's coast cause tidal ebbing and flowing over great stretches. Most capes and headlands however, drop steeply into the depths and all that is exposed at extreme ebb tide is just more rock – rocks that have been chiseled, flattened or contorted by countless years of battering. River bars, inlets and dogholes often produce strong currents on the ebb tides and especially where large rivers enter the ocean.

Oceanographers claim that if the entire Pacific Coast was as straight as an arrow with a smooth offshore shelf, the tides would advance along its entire mass with constant speeds and menacing inundation of land masses. God, the master creator, saw to it that the Oregon shoreline was a mixture of promontories, curving sandy beaches and pincushions of rocky outcrops that keep the whole process pretty much in line and makes a habitable wonderland for both the creatures of the land and the creatures of the sea.

Few there are who at one time have not pondered the mystery of the waves. This potential source of energy is not quite what it appears to be. It isn't that each wave as an entity is traveling over a long distance, but a pulsating action passing through the water. A glass fishing float, a bottle or pieces of drift can travel long distances at the whim of current and wind but the waves just appear to be water on the way to somewhere else – like potential energy moving in a visible form. A sizable wave can travel upward to 5,000 miles, enough to cross any ocean in the world.

At the outset, the waves are created when a sea breeze blowing over the surface causes ripples to form as a result of friction, much in the same manner as throwing a rock into a still millpond and watching it send out a series of little ripples that widen and grow until they reach the shores of the pond. Storms usually start a confused wave pattern but nearly always have a general direction. When the waves outrun the wind, they settle into the regular height and spacing of open ocean swells the pattern often leading to that old nemesis of the sea *mal de mer*. Many a landlubber, on testing the elevator of the billows personally, has longed for *terra firma*.

No more of the sea, enough for me!
   I'm green at the gills, despite my pills,
Oh for dry land, a step on the sand,
   Oh me oh my, I think I'll die.

Sick, yes I am, please get me a pan,
   The pitch and the roll is taking its toll,
Just put me ashore, and forever more,
   I'll live out my days in landlubber ways.

Waves are constant at sea but when the energy stored within touches the shallow shelf leading to the beaches, surf is created and the energy uncovered yields a spectacular climax. The original height of the wave determines how far offshore the surf zone begins during any prevailing conditions. As the wave gets to the shallow areas, its front edge slows quicker than its hind zone, the column compresses, the wave gets thinner and taller, becomes unstable and then collapses. Thus, the death of a wave.

Oceanographers tell us that gently shoaling beaches do not produce, as a rule, crashing surf, as the wave energy is spent with bottom friction being extremely lessened. Wide surf zones on the other hand produce a labyrinth of troughs and sandbars that have larger breakers on the outer bar and smaller ones on the inner side. If, on the other hand, the approach to the outer bar is steep, then plunging breakers are the result. Succeeding waves are lesser but culminate in an unpredictable mixture of plunging and spilling breakers. Steep approaches to a beach will bring waves right up to the termination of life when they suddenly well-up and crash-down in a frightening, exciting show of violence.

One can virtually tell the topography of a beach by these simple rules:

1. Green water is deep
2. White water is shallow
3. Spilling breakers mean gentle slope
4. Plunging breakers designate steep slope.
5. Three or four lines of breakers indicate several parallel sand bars with intervening troughs.

Of course, such a measuring stick is not entirely accurate because weather and sea conditions on the Oregon coast can

Cleft-of-the-Rock Lighthouse south of Yachats, can be seen from the southbound side of the highway.

confuse the general rule at any time. During adverse weather, the entire shoreline can become white-lipped fury from north to south as far as the eye can see.

Knowing the topography of the sea was a science to the early Polynesian navigators who explored and settled the myriad of islands of the Pacific as far east as Hawaii and Easter Island. But the southern ocean is not like the North Pacific Ocean. Frequent overcast days and changing cloud patterns reflect on the ocean's face. The menu of the day in the South Pacific is generally clear, sunny skies affording the sea a steady variety of hues – blues, aquamarine, greens – each revealing the controlling depths.

To repeat, despite all the books that have been written about the sea, its mystery, intrigue and attraction continue to grow in the mortal mind.

The Oregon coast, often peaceful, occasionally violent, is certainly not an exception.

> James A. "Jim" Gibbs
> Cleft-of-the-Rock Lighthouse
> Cape Perpetua
> Yachats, Oregon

Southbound travelers on U. S. Highway 101 will cross the lower reach of Cape Perpetua providing a spectacular view of the Pacific Ocean. A side road leads to this viewpoint. Highway 101 follows the coastline and provides access to beachcombing opportunities, state parks and lighthouses as well as to most of the primary coastal communities.

20

Chapter 1
Cape Perpetua, A Good Place To Start

What better place to discover the Oregon coast than at its midpoint, the crown of the central sector, Cape Perpetua. This precipitous monolith rising 803 feet a short distance from the beach and over 1,000 feet within ¾th of a mile, is the highest immediately fronting the coast. Rising sharply from the sea, it was forged in the furnace of the earth, spewed out as molten lava and formed as a bastion to stand for time immemorial as a warlike castle fending off the charging seas that constantly roll against its girth.

Since its inception, the Eocene basalts (hard, dark-colored rock of volcanic origin) have weathered the onslaught of wind, wave and torrent. For most of the eons of time it knew not the footprints of man. Long before white explorers' sails broke the horizon, occasional coastal Indian villages dotted the shoreline. Great shell mounds, residue of the ravenous feasting on shellfish and game are all that remain of a people that lived in relative peace in a happy fishing and hunting ground which in their ignorance was tantamount to Eden itself. Illiterate, yet satisfied, one generation paralleling the next, their culture remained primitive, but stable. Completely unaware of the existence of the white man and his progressive ways, and without contact from the outside world, those natives, like the early Polynesians, pursued the only kind of an existence they knew. And they found it wasn't all that bad. They fished, they hunted, they bartered, they lived, they died.

Occasionally, rival tribes on the Central Oregon coast would war against one another, usually when one invaded the territory of the other. Skirmishes were generally short-lived. Their eventual demise came with the white man who was to bring disease,

Oregon Coast Highway 101 near Heceta Head. The hand-built rock walls were projects of the Civilian Conservation Corps in the 1930's..

whiskey, guns and superior power. Once under subjugation, the Indians were herded onto reservations as a result of misguided federal policy.

Ancient Indians revered the lands that spread out in the shadow of Perpetua south to the Siuslaw and northward to the Alsea and Yaquina Rivers. In the lee of the great promontory flowed a myriad of streams, including the peaceful Yachats River, two miles north of the cape. In this general area lived probably no more contented red men in America. They had everything to sustain life for a primitive people – an endless abundance of game, fish, roots, berries and shellfish. The largest shell mounds found anyplace in Oregon were discovered at Yachats and on Cape Perpetua. There is hardly a section where one cannot dig into the ground and hit layers of shells where Indians sat by the hour and gorged themselves on a continuing supply of mussels,

Astoria Bridge crosses the Columbia River. Washington is in the background. This bridge formed the final link in Highway 101. Picture was made on opening day in 1966.

Yaquina Bay Bridge, Newport. This view is from Yaquina Bay lighthouse.

23

clams and oysters.

With relatively mild weather the year-round, and a constant fresh supply of pure scintillating water, tall timber and beaches choked with driftwood, it is hard to imagine a more idyllic situation for a primitive race.

Probably they roamed there for well over a thousand years. Had not the white man come, their simple, unchangeable way of life would have perhaps continued for countless decades just as prior to the age of exploration.

Tribes prominent along the Oregon coast were the Clatsop, Tillamook, Alsi, Siuslaw, Coos, Tututni, Chetco and Umpqua.*

Today, the descendants of the central coast Indians are mostly settled in the Siletz area, northeast of Newport, while a ribbon of black asphalt winds along the coast – Highway 101 – through their old familiar haunts. Since the early 1930's, millions of vehicles from the old Model T Fords to the fanciest Cadillac of the present day have brought countless tourists to view Oregon's sea front. Caucasian residents have occupied virtually all of the favorite haunts of the ancient Indian. The trip along the Oregon coast a half century ago demanded the crossing of the major coastal rivers by pint-sized ferryboats whose limited services were terminated with the completion of the highway bridges.**

Cape Perpetua, in the extreme southwest corner of Lincoln County, is not only prominent but historic. Discovered on March 7, 1778 by Captain James Cook, the intrepid English sea rover, explorer and navigator, it remains an eternal sentinel to his honor. Some misguided historians attribute the name of the cape to the nasty weather Cook encountered which "perpetually" kept him within its view. According to the navigator's journal, however, he named the headland for St. Perpetua, an early Christian martyr

---

*For complete description of these tribes including village locations, language groups, etc., refer to *Indians Along the Oregon Trail; The Tribes of Nebraska, Wyoming, Idaho, Oregon and Washington Identified* see bibliography.

**The Coast Highway was completed except for its major bridges by 1932. By 1938 all of the great bridges were in place. These were at Newport, Waldport, Florence, Coos Bay, Gold Beach. The famous Alsea Bridge was declared obsolete and unsafe in the 1980's and was replaced in 1992. The highest bridge in all of Oregon is on the coast, the 345-feet high Thomas Creek Bridge on Highway 101 in Curry County. It was constructed in 1961. The Columbia River Bridge at Astoria, at four miles (21,474 feet) long, is Oregon's longest bridge. This bridge was opened in 1966.

allegedly murdered in Carthage on March 7, in the year 203. It was on that day in 1778, (once celebrated in old England), that Cook sighted the cape.

Wandering through or inhabiting the wilds of the cape and of the 622,000 acre Siuslaw National Forest, are varieties of animals: raccoons, squirrels, chipmunks, black bear, black-tailed deer and elk. On the sea front, seabirds of most every type from the seagull to the pelican, from the cormorant to the sandpiper and from the murre to the oyster catcher, dine on fish and crustaceans and nest on the steep slopes. In the depths, live everything from the slippery little smelt to the great gray whale which travels as far as 11,000 miles annually between the Arctic Ocean and Mexico. They parade off the Central Oregon coast, some leaving the migratory route to stay on for a considerable while. These leviathans, some bettering 50 feet, weigh a ton per foot and make the longest ocean migration of any of the whale species. Uncanny in their navigational instincts, they perform through the sea what the swallows accomplish in their annual junket to Capistrano.

There is life everywhere on the sea front. On the rocks exposed on the ebbing of the tides, is a carpet of blue mussels by the millions interspersed with voracious barnacles. There are starfish of virtually every color of the rainbow and the ever present green sea anemones that close up when exposed by the tide and open like delicate flowers when inundated. Deceptive, they attract, anesthetize and entrap their victims in their folding petals. Some of the larger anemones live to be 150 years old enjoying twice the life span of humans. Then there are the defiant sea palms, another strange marine plant organism that is shaped almost like a miniature palm tree, shackling themselves in the most unbelievable places where the full power of the breakers smashes against exposed rock. They take the punishment of hundreds of super bowl linemen and only occasionally get decapitated.

Dotted with giant spruce which breast the howling winds of winter, Cape Perpetua stands almost as a symbol similar to the other great headlands that front the Oregon coast. Often times the forces of nature send storm waves smashing against her girdle of rock, her trees being rudely extracted by howling blasts of wind that sometimes climb to the top of the Beaufort scale. The countless marine creatures compete for a place to dwell. Unseen micro-organisms relentlessly turn fallen vegetation into soil while rocks, pounded loose from the cliff sides, many of the agate variety, fall onto the beaches to be polished by the sluicing waves into fascinating semi-precious gems. There are also bloodstones and jasper.

> **Be Alert To Possible Injury**
> Fissures and sea caves, as well as the ebb and flow of uneven unpredictable breaker patterns, may provide a fascination for the human. But yearly, as has been told, many are injured and sometimes killed by not using precautions. In recent years, a teenager fell into one of the many caves between Yachats and Cape Perpetua. Barreling waves roared through the cave's mouth enveloping the boy time after time. Only the unusual formation of the cave permitted his ability to breath occasional air. Those who came to rescue him were forced to lower a member of the rescue squad through a small hole at the top. The breakers were soon snapping at him as he swung like a pendulum in a gale. He was drenched by the crashing sea several times, finally reaching the youth. By superhuman effort both were hoisted free of danger.

One must also beware of the drift logs responsible for injury and sometimes death. Breakers can knock the unsuspecting from a log which in turn rolls over him or catch him in a scissors-like action in conjunction with a second log. Running on logs or jumping from log-to-log is an accident looking for a place to happen.

There is a huge sea cave directly under the highest slope of Perpetua. Chiseled out of a basaltic mass by onrushing surf through countless years, the cavity, like a small amphitheater, is nearly 50 feet high and 100 feet deep. During the winter storms the effect is sensational as seas roar to the butt end of the cave then cascade back out, regurgitating tons of white spray in geyser-like proportions. □

Chapter 2
The Discovery of Sea Lion Cave

When it comes to sea caves, none is greater than the Sea Lion Cave, claimed to be the world's largest. Located ten miles south of Cape Perpetua, the place has been an official tourist attraction since 1932. With a floor area of nearly two acres and a vaulted rock dome some 125 feet high southward from the main chamber, a low passage runs 1,000 feet to a sea level opening. Measured from another direction the cave is nearly 1,500 feet long blending in its cathedral-like ceiling hues of greens, pinks, reds and purples. The colors reflect in the ocean water inside the cave sometimes producing a beautiful aquamarine color not un-like the Blue Grotto on Italy's Isle of Capri.

Not in the British Isles, New Zealand or Japan has there been found a cave of comparable size and interest. But of course the cave itself is not the main attraction, it being the stellar sea lions that make it their home.

Tourists enter 320 feet above sea level, and are taken into the cave in an elevator to the floor of the cave where they, at the right season, find hundreds of these great mammals from playful 30 pound pups to ornery and powerful one ton bulls posing a threat to any would-be trespassers. Content to stay inside or outside their unique natural habitat the year round, these cumbersome creatures have found a perfect environment. When the weather is pleasant and mild, they fish, frolic and sunbathe on the rocks outside the cave. During adverse weather they have at their disposal the full and complete protection of perhaps the best animal hideaway in all the world. Inside the cave are three openings: two facing the sea and one "dry" entrance to the north. In 1932, a footpath and a stairway with 111 steps gave entry to the cave.

The elevator which now descends to the cave floor is a far cry from the entrance made by the adventurous seafarer who discovered the indenture in the coastal wall in 1880. This was William Cox, a retired sea captain. As long as there are things to be discovered, man will try, or die in the attempt. Captain Cox was such an individual. He was determined to discover what was inside the deceptive entrance. Perhaps he had visions of finding some ancient Spanish treasure, loot from a captured galleon hidden within by a band of swarthy pirates. Even then such legends were persistent along the Oregon coast. Again, maybe he visualized a terrifying sea serpent or perhaps a mermaid combing her lovely locks on the slippery rocks inside the entrance. Whatever his dreams, he was intrigued by the presence of the cave and laid plans to enter it by skiff there being no known way to gain entrance to the cave from the landside. An experienced hand with a small boat, he was willing to challenge the rise and fall of the swell pulsating at the cave entrance. Sizing up the situation, Cox, his heart in his mouth, proceeded. His craft lifted and then settled in the trough. Arm and back muscles straining, he endeavored to keep from broaching to and capsizing. Through the entrance, a swell caught the boat and pushed it forward and the outside light was suddenly diffused. As his eyes adjusted, he looked about in total amazement at the size and extent of this unusual cavern. Lighting a kerosene lantern, he held it aloft and searched for a place to land the boat. Finding a gentle, sloping rock shelf, he made it fast and began his exploration of the weird shapes and shadowed corners, his heart pounding at being the first white man to enter the strange, hidden domain. If any of the coastal Indians had entered, it was a well guarded secret for they believed such places to be full of evil spirits. Perhaps Cox was the first human to explore the cave.

His fascination drew attention away from a few sea lions scattered about. Upset by the presence of this intruder, they barked but to no avail. Further, Cox had paid little attention to a mounting surf, foaming and curling at the entrance. When ready to leave, his passageway out was blocked! The adventurer was trapped! The weather, though calm on the inside, had soured on the outside and the ocean was being whipped into a furious froth.

A storm was in the making.

Pondering his seemingly foolhardy adventure, Cox resigned himself to settle down with his sea lion companions until conditions would permit his exit. How long, he wondered, would it be until he saw the full light of day again. The poor captain was in a bit of a predicament to say the least. He was getting hunger pangs and he was cold. The surf continued to pant angrily at the cave entrance as if daring him to venture forth. Hours passed. It was a long interlude before the storm died and the seas calmed to where he believed he might get out. Finally, the desperate individual made his daring exit, this time heading directly into the surf. Hands tightly gripped on the oars, the doughty captain stubbornly pulled the craft back out into what seemed a great, big beautiful world uninhibited by rock walls.

For such an exploit it would seem that history would have preserved the occasion by officially naming this geographic feature Cox Cave. Alas, the sea lions whose home it has been for decades were accorded the honor.

But don't feel too bad for Mr. Cox for he was not entirely overlooked. His name was applied to a prominent seamark, a mile and a half south of Heceta Head, a conical-shaped hunk of basalt. Evidently the birds have not respected Cox's sentinel as they continue to whiten its summit and sides with their droppings. □

Heceta Head, 28.5 miles N of Umpqua River Light, has a seaward face 2.5 miles long with nearly vertical cliffs 100 to 200 feet high. The summit of the head reaches an elevation of 1,000 feet 0.5 mile from the cliffs and is covered with grass and a few pines. A sharp black conical rock, 180 feet high, marks the extreme W and N part of the head, and is easily made out from either N or S. **Cox Rock,** 1.5 miles S of the S part of the head, is conical and usually white on top with bird droppings. —United States Coast Pilot, Pacific Coast.

Chapter 3
Heceta Head

Picturesque Heceta Head, probably closer to the half-way mark on the Oregon coast than Perpetua, lies only a mile north of the Sea Lion Cave. It was named for the renowned Spanish ship-master and explorer Bruno Heceta, commanding the corvette *Santiago*. Perhaps the most photographed and painted geographical feature on the coast, its basic popularity is attributed to the picturesque and thought-provoking lighthouse so perfectly set into the seascape. One almost feels it has been there since the beginning of time.

When the *Santiago* passed the bold headland in the late summer of 1775, it was probably observed by wide-eyed Indians filled with both excitement and terror. Brer' Bruno, however, wasn't quite so impressed, scanning the misty shoreline as he did, noting shallow water for some distance off the cape suggesting for the sake of a better name, Heceta Bank. Though the cape bears his name, he might have gained far greater fame had he ventured into the Columbia River, historians claiming that he was actually the first to recognize its existence. He saw the Columbia, the long sought after "River of the West" on August 17, 1775, noting an opening from which rushed a current so strong he could not enter. Had he waited for the bar to calm and crossed over, history would read considerably different. Instead, the great discovery was left to a Yankee, Robert Gray, who on May 11, 1792 entered the river and named it for his ship the *Columbia Rediviva*. Heceta's nautical observations placed his position within one minute of the latitude of Cape Disappointment at the river's north side which he named Cape San Roque, before breezing onward to other dis-coveries.

(**←Left page**) Heceta Head Lighthouse seen from Scenic View Area on south-bound side of highway 101. Many proclaim this is the most photographed view in all of Oregon. The lighthouse was rededicated during an Open House on April 2 - 3, 1994.

31

About the Discovery of the Columbia River

The commanders of the voyages of discovery along the Northwest Coast had been at sea for a longtime. What caused some of these men to fail to make significant discoveries? Is it possible they were tired and had lost their enthusiasm?

Captain Cook found his ship enveloped by fog and didn't stay long enough for the fog to lift. What might he have seen if he had?

Vancouver: While he was out there sailing around, did he really look close enough when he was near the Columbia River?

And the Spanish: Some turned back because of scurvy. Why didn't they put to shore to seek something fresh to eat then set out again?

The Columbia's entrance can be hard to find thus early explorers passed within a few leagues and never saw it. The Spanish, British, Portuguese, French, Dutch and Russians all passed by – missed it.

Bartolome Ferrelo had long heard rumors of such a river and Sir Francis Drake apparently didn't go far enough on his voyage of 1579. Apostolos Valerianos, under the name Juan de Fuca, sailed on north and discovered the strait that separates the United States from Canada that bears his name. But he missed the Columbia River.

Some of these men appeared timid of the line of breakers off the bar and wouldn't chance standing by for clear weather then being adventurous and make the crossing. Such was Bruno Heceta in the *Santiago*. Back at headquarters, the Spanish authorities were displeased that he had not pushed just a little harder, so they did not tell anybody of the plausibility that Heceta may have stood off the mouth of a great river but had not entered it.

Then there is Robert Gray. In 1792, Gray had his mind on securing beaver skins and not on discovering the greatest river of the Northwest Coast. He saw the same line of breakers at the Columbia River's bar as did some others, but he, with possibility thinking and an uncanny sixth sense, waited around then worked his ship over the bar and gained the river. Gray was a quiet man and did not grandstand his discovery. But he did tell other sea captains what he'd found and they caused his discovery to be entered on navigation charts.

Robert Gray in his ship, the *Columbia Rediviva,* made history and established an interest in the Oregon Country for the United States. The young U. S. A. would prove to be a power to be dealt with.

With the discovery of the great River of the West, it did not take long for mariners to start using it. Hazardous bar, dangerous currents, the losses of hundreds of ships of all sizes at or near the bar, has never deterred man from crossing it. The river has always been included in discussions of the Oregon Coast because not only does it form this coast's northern border at the sea, but the commerce on the river has involved the coast as well.

32

The Oregon coast, in the age of exploration and up through the coming of the white settlers, was divided by its prominent headlands. These great landmarks were the only means of locating the respective parts of the shoreline. We know them today as Tillamook Head; Mt. Neah-kah-nie; Cape Meares; Cape Lookout, Cascade Head; Cape Foulweather; Cape Perpetua; Heceta Head: Cape Arago: Cape Blanco; Humbug Mountain; Cape Sebastian; Cape Ferrelo.

All are prominent and rise directly from the ocean shores. All of these natural sentinels served at one time or another as landfalls. The galleons returning from the exotic east as early as the 16th century set their inbound courses by these headlands in accordance with the winds that waited them after crossing the vast Pacific.

Occasionally, the similarity of these capes and headlands from the seaward side caused mistaken identity which led to many erroneous calculations in the faded past. □

Yaquina Bay Bridge, Highway 101. View is toward the south.

33

Chapter 4
Explorers, Wrecked Ships, Treasure and Bees Wax

Is there a subject that so ignites the excitement and imagination as that of buried treasure? When one thinks of old Spain, gold, silver and precious stones immediately come to mind. Where there was Spanish treasure, not far behind were pirates thirsting for plunder in the name of lust, greed, fame, fortune or prestige.

> **The Age of Discovery**
> The fantastic Oregon Coast was discovered due to the orderly progression of world explorations led by the likes of Magellan, Balboa, Drake, Juan de Fuca, Ferrelo, Cook, and a few others. Here is how it all fits together.

That the ships of wealthy Spain were usually the target of marauders may seem unjustified, but when one considers the larger share of Spain's wealth was ruthlessly extracted from Aztecs, Incas, Indians, Southeast Asians and others, under the guise of religion, perhaps it was just retribution.

Aside from the subject of treasure, the brave, intrepid Spanish navigators of past centuries deserve much credit for opening unknown seas and lands to world commerce long before other nations dared venture far from their home waters. To pioneer the hidden corners of the world they suffered much hardship and privation. Shipwreck was common and the dreaded scurvy wiped out Spanish sailors by the score. Though they wielded a mighty sword over many of their victims, the price they paid in human life was considerable.

Mouth of Columbia River and Astoria Bridge seen from top the Astor Tower on Coxcomb Hill. The tower, open to the public, is 125 feet tall.

Though much of the discovery of the new world must properly go to the Vikings, the Portuguese, the Dutch, English, French and Russians, yet it was Spain that stood out, especially where the Pacific was concerned. Spanish sailors of old were not strangers to Oregon's prominent coastal landmarks.

Of course, due to the astounding research of New Zealand-born Bary Fell, a marine biologist, much of the accepted early history may be changed. The Harvard researcher has come up with a deciphering of an ancient language affording strong evidence that there were men and women from Europe not merely exploring, but living in North America as early as 800 B. C. They worked as miners, tanners and trappers, and are believed to have shipped their products back to Europe. Celtic and Carthaginian people, pagan worshippers of Baal, lived, worked and traded in New England and in the mid-west, their only monuments some strange haunts, one reputedly a winter solstice chamber in Vermont, believed to have been used by New England Celts for lunar observations, and a series of slab stone buildings in New

Hampshire.

A great lapse in history must have occurred, and the contact between two continents was abruptly terminated for, until recent years, most of our exploration type history books revolved around America's discovery by Christopher Columbus in 1492.

Whatever new historical discoveries might be uncovered, Spain will continue to remain as a Pacific pioneer, though antedated by the Polynesians. Unfortunately this great nation of yesteryear sought power through wealth, and this ultimately helped cause her downfall. The cost of exploration had yielded little in the early 16th century. In 1519, Spanish royalty, bogged down with internal affairs enlisted the services of the intrepid Ferdinand Magellan, a renowned Portuguese navigator whose country had refused his grandiose plans for new world discovery. By royal edict, he, with a picked crew was dispatched to seek a passage around South America to the East Indies, a demanding voyage that was to end in triumph, hardship and tragedy.

Spain had rejected the magnitude of Columbus' discovery of the West Indies and the fact that he proved the world was not flat. He had unknowingly opened a whole new future world of wealth for Mother Spain, but he, one of the world's great explorers, was to die in disgrace.

Before Magellan's epic voyage, Balboa had already crossed the Isthmus to discover the Great South Sea, naming it "Pacific," in 1513, while Portuguese explorers had sailed eastward terminating with the Oriental world. To Magellan fell the task of rounding, for the first time, the whole of South America and clawing his way with a fleet of small vessels. These were the *Trinidad, Santiago, San Antonio, Concepcion and Victoria.* All set out from Sanlucar, Spain on September 20, 1519 to cross the great oceans on the boldest voyage of discovery ever attempted. He was to discover an "outlet to the Moluccas" through which trade would inevitably follow.

It took three months for the fleet to reach Rio de Janeiro after which Magellan pressed southward toward ice-laced Antarctica. Then the *Santiago,* sent southward to reconnoiter, was wrecked. The *San Antonio* was sent home when the pilot refused to go further. The three remaining ships proceeded through what we know today as the Strait of Magellan, the high-walled desolate wastes that cut through the toe of South America. After rigorous days of terrible suffering, they reached the vast Pacific Ocean,* and sailed along the coast of Chile finally turning westward in the Pacific toward the Spice Islands.

Week after week they sailed the wide ocean until their water and food supply was exhausted, the crews subsisting on sawdust and leather strapping from the rigging. Scurvy and beri beri took their toll. Finally, an abandoned atoll was reached for temporary replenishment. However, by March 5, 1521, the food supply was exhausted once again. Just then suddenly appeared the island we know today as Guam. Here they found what seemed a Utopia: coconuts, sugar cane and bananas, the latter being the favorite, as many of the men had lost their teeth from scurvy.

Following recuperation and replenishment, Magellan sailed to the meridian of the Philippine archipelago in the cause of discovery. He landed at tiny Limasawa, then went on to other islands where he influenced many pagan people to adopt the Roman Catholic faith. He, however, came up against a stubborn chief named Mactan who, with his followers, surrounded Magellan and stabbed him to death.

The expedition leader, having circumnavigated the world, had opened the future ocean track that Spanish ships would follow for the next two and a half centuries.

The remaining ships, *Trinidad and Victoria* (the *Concepcion* had earlier burned) withdrew to East Indies, spice ports. Only the battered, leaking *Victoria* made it home under the command of Juan Sebastian del Cano. Of the original 247 man expedition, only 18 were to complete the circumnavigation of the world – a three year voyage which ended Sept. 8, 1522.

*   *   *

Now, the reader may ask, what does Magellan's voyage have

---

* For an account of the most famous voyage through the Strait of Magellan, other than that of Ferdinand Magellan, in history, refer to *Battleship Oregon, Bulldog of the Navy*. In 1898, the battleship's speed run from San Francisco to Florida, under forced draught, set records never surpassed. On arrival, the ship reported for duty in the Spanish-American War and when the running sea battle opened, the *Oregon* out-ran, out-shot all other ships of both navies. See bibliography.

to do with Oregon? First, it revealed the Americas as a separate continent from Asia. Second and probably more important, it opened Spanish transpacific trade that was to last for two and a half centuries. The route connected the western rim of North America with the Orient or, as the Spanish put it, trade between New Spain (Mexico), the Philippines, East Indies and Moluccas.

Through this period, Oregon territory was virtually unknown to the civilized world, but under the beach sands and rocky outcrops of the Oregon coast are believed to be the rotting remains of both Spanish galleons once engaged in the transpacific trade and of caravels sailing up the coast from Mexico.

With the route established, a galleon made the passage from Spain to the East Indies annually. On the westbound trek, the cumbersome sailing vessels would fall in with the prevailing winds and currents near the equator, then northward to Magellan's old anchorage in Los Ladrones (Guam), then on to Manila. On the eastward voyage, the galleons would set a northerly course catching the prevailing winds falling in with the Japanese Current. By turning east at the northerly end of the Japanese archipelago, The ships followed the great circle route across the Pacific. This put the vessels in the far north Pacific Ocean near Alaska, then south toward Oregon on the California Current. Though a landfall was sought along the northern California coast, usually Cape Mendocino, storms, fickle wind and currents could bring a landfall anywhere between the 30th and 46th parallel (south of Enseñada, Mexico to the north Oregon coast).

Generally, after a long eastbound passage, any headland from northern California to northern Oregon was acceptable for determining one's tentative position before working south along the coast to Acapulco or San Blas. Storm-wracked ships also found refuge at Monterey or the bays of San Francisco and San Diego. Much of the trouble faced by ship captains came from the contrary seas and the fog-shrouded coast of Oregon.

History has paid little mind to it, but it appears that Sir Francis Drake, first Englishman to circumnavigate the world, (1577-1580) anchored for five days in June of 1579 in the cove on the south side of Oregon's Cape Arago. He too, complained of a "vile stinking fogge." To show his contempt for Oregon coast

Sir Francis Drake first saw the Pacific Ocean from the top of a mountain in Panama in 1572. The next year he left England with five ships but only one, the *Golden Hind*, cruised the California and Oregon coasts. Drake did not land in Oregon but complained of the offshore "stinking fogge."

weather, he named it "Bad Bay."

For a half century after Ferrelo's reputed sighting of Oregon, no known official exploration northward was attempted by Spain. Instead, Spain's attention was directed toward the Orient where it was confidently anticipated that rich provinces might be secured.

Hernando Cortez who landed in Mexico, as early as 1519, had not been oblivious to the wealth of the Far East for in 1525 he sent two ships with the object of taking the Philippine Islands. The expedition failed but a second, under Ruy Lopez de Villabos, with the backing of a large force was successful in taking the islands. Later, however, he was forced into relinquishing control through native reprisal.

Not until 1564 were the Spanish totally successful in their efforts due to the leadership of Miguel de Legazpi. He had sailed from Mexico with a considerable number of militiamen and a large fleet of ships. He was to enforce Spain's claim to the coveted archipelago. Spain was to hold a sword over the islands for the next 300 years, extracting countless quantities in gold, silver and precious gems to fatten the coffers of Spanish royalty.

In Legazpi's expedition sailed one Urdanata who, though acting as a priest, was an excellent navigator. It was he who officially noted for the first time that the trade winds blew always in one direction within certain limits on both sides of the equator. This made it easy to sail west but that route was be avoided on the eastward track. He sailed northward into a region where the winds would be more variable. On his recommendation, the fleet

The North Pacific coastline as of 1795 drawn by J. Russel. He was oblivious to Gray's discovery of the Columbia River which he named Deception Bay at the river's mouth. He called today's Tillamook Bay, "Quicksand Bay."

on its eastward trip, sailed north to the 40th parallel permitting a passage with far less difficulty. This was to become the accepted route of the galleons which, with favoring winds, could usually make a landfall somewhere near Cape Mendocino before following the coast southward.

A profitable trade resulted between Manila and Acapulco. The early caravels gave way to larger more commodious, stronger built galleons as Spain now considered the Pacific Ocean its own exclusive lake, even forbidding other countries from its waters.

When Dutch and English ships later defied that dictum, Spain labeled the intruders "illegitimate pirates." If Spain captured any of these vessels, its crewmen were hung immediately from the highest yardarm.

Spain held the coveted "throne" of trade. The greed for wealth under the cloak of conquest and religion produced many unfortunate overtones but it took a long time to dethrone the king of the seas. What was the influence on Oregon?

Many of the salts of the old Spanish galleons gazed upon the shores of Oregon on returning from the Orient but who actually was the first Caucasian to see Oregon's virgin coast? One must remember that in the early years, navigation instruments were crude at best, sightings were subject to question, and explorers were apt to fudge a little about their accomplishments.

Was the discoverer of Oregon, d'Aguilar, Ferrelo, Flores or Viscaino? How about the old Greek mariner Valerianos, who sailed for Spain by using the name Juan de Fuca? He told Michael Lok, respected English merchant living in Venice in April 1596, of having been in the West Indies of Spain for 40 years. Further he claimed to have been in a Spanish vessel returning from the "Islands Philippinas," toward "Nova España" which was plundered and taken at "Cape California" by Captain Candish (Cavendish), whereby he lost 60,000 ducats of his own goods.

Also he claimed, the viceroy sent him out again in 1592 with only a small caravel and a pinnace armed with mariners only, to try to discover of the Strait of Anian and the passage thereof into the sea. He followed his course in that voyage west and northwest in the South Sea, (North Pacific) all along the coast of Nova Spania and California, and the Indies (along the Oregon Coast) until he came to latitude 47 degrees. That's the latitude of Aberdeen, Washington. There, finding that land trended north and northeast, with a broad inlet of sea, between 47 and 48 degrees of latitude, he entered sailing more than 20 days. Before entering that strait, he sighted:

...a great headland or island [Cape Flattery] with an exceeding high pinnacle [Fuca's Pillar] or spired rock like a pillar thereupon.

The Strait of Juan de Fuca still bears his name despite the efforts of numerous historians to discredit his claim. Neither do any documents about his alleged discovery exist in the Spanish archives but then, of course, the loosely operated government of New Spain paid little heed to the discovery aspect unless treasure was involved.

41

If de Fuca's account is true, he and Sir Francis Drake may have been the first white explorers to sail along the coast of Oregon.

It is obvious that there was considerable Spanish maritime activity along the Pacific Northwest shores in pre-discovery times. The evidence speaks for itself. In addition to early Spanish and oriental shipwrecks along the Oregon coast, Indian legend claims that a vessel was wrecked near the Quinault River in Washington as early as 1550.

Never did a galleon depart Manila without a cargo of treasure – gold, silver, spices, as well as such items as rare silks, taffeta, Cantonese crepes, costly vestments for cathedral priests. There were precious cut and uncut stones, fabulous jewelry, costly gifts from India's mogul and highly prized Ghedda wax. This was a beeswax common to India and utilized by the Roman church for tapers and candles. Why a market for this wax over any other variety? It burned better – slower.

Often "sized" for galleon transport, many chunks of beeswax were inscribed with numerals over which historians disagree as to meaning to the present day. Tons of Ghedda beeswax have been removed from the sands along the Oregon coast particularly from the south entrance of the Columbia River to and beyond Nehalem Spit. If a beachcomber is lucky, some can be still found at the present time. The largest discovery in recent years was at Nehalem Beach near Manzanita in 1973. This was a 45 pound piece discovered in the sands by Lowell Damon.

Tons of the wax, perhaps well over 300 tons have reputedly come from at least one wreck of a Spanish vessel on Nehalem Beach. Indians told of such an incident long before the white settlers came to Oregon. Oriental junks also carried beeswax but the quantities were not nearly so large. It is however, a fact that junks did wreck on Oregon beaches in ancient times and perhaps may have left an additional amount of the wax to help confuse the modern mind as to its source.

From the initial transpacific crossings of Manila caravels and galleons, commencing in 1565 until the final voyage in 1815, records in Spanish archives list 30 of these vessels as having been lost on Pacific passages.

Examples of a number of pieces of beeswax recovered from the area of Nehalem Bay State Park are exhibited in Tillamook Pioneer Museum and, as shown here, in the Manzanita City Hall.

Most of this number went to a watery grave in the fickle, often hazardous Philippine Sea. One is known to have stranded on the inhospitable rocks of a Japanese island. Still another was captured and plundered by a British privateer and two others disappeared at sea. Of the latter, one is traditionally believed to have been wrecked off San Miguel Island (in the Channel group) off California's coast. This is because traces of Ghedda beeswax has been found there. Some believe this ship to have been the *San Antonio*, a treasure-laden craft that departed from Manila in 1603. Another, the *San Augustin*, is known to have been wrecked in Drakes Bay in California in 1595.

Another galleon that failed to make port was the *San Francisco Xavier*, claimed by many to be the wreck on Nehalem Beach near Manzanita. If so, it was cast ashore in 1705. Generations of Nehalem Indians extracted its beeswax from the beaches, as eventually did the whites after they arrived.

As New Spain dispatched smaller caravel-type supply vessels up the coast to California seeking new harbors of refuge for

Here is Lowell Damon's 45-pound chunk of beeswax
he discovered in 1973 on Nehalem beach.

The Never Ending Mystery of the Beeswax

The majority of treasure-seekers are convinced that the Oregon
beeswax probably came from the galleon *San Francisco Xavier*. The
vessel had been on the Manila to Mexico trade route when it was blown
off course and was wrecked on the Oregon beach near Manzanita. In the
1930's, Waldeman H. Hollenstad of Manzanita found a unique piece of
wax marked with a cross in a circle. The piece is about 15 by 18 inches
and between 4 and 5 inches thick. Hollenstad and his wife, Helen, used
the piece as a mantel decoration for many years. It is now in a showcase
in the Manzanita City Hall. Radio carbon-dating claims it was formed
about 1681 with the shipwreck between 1700 and 1710. A dead bee was
found in the wax. The U.S. Geological Survey states the wax was formed
by bees. It is estimated that about 10 tons of beeswax has been uncovered between Cape Meares and Tillamook Head.

—Data courtesy of Wayne Jensen, Director, Tillamook Pioneer Museum

Remains of heavy beam of hardwood, beachcombed by Burford Wilkerson in 1950's, is believed by some to be from a Spanish galleon.

returning galleons, as well as for establishing missions, some were swept northward to the Oregon coast by the great southwest gales, never to return to their ports of departure. It is not only possible but probably quite correct to assume that some of these craft were cast ashore on Oregon beaches and entered in the viceroy's ledger as, "lost without trace."

The northward movement of caravels goes way back. Cape Ferrelo on Oregon's southern coast was reputedly named by Bartolome Ferrelo, who was Cabrillo's pilot in 1542 and 1543. (This was just a half century after Columbus crossed the Atlantic Ocean.) Cabrillo died en route but his final words to Ferrelo were to continue north. Ferrelo did just that but the cape, as many historians insist, may not be the one he actually saw. On Jan. 19, 1543, Ferrelo carried out his dying commander's instructions by sailing northward in the teeth of a gale. He gained 42 degrees 30 minutes on March 1 only a breath away from Cape Blanco (42° 50' 14"N) which would have to wait another 59 years before being officially discovered.

Ferrelo's ship ran out of food, his crew was down with scurvy, thus he had no choice but to come about and return home.

Some historians argue that Juan Rodriguez Cabrillo had only reached the 38th parallel when he succumbed, a little north of San Francisco Bay, and that his counterpart, Ferrelo, got only as far as Cape Mendocino and was not the first white explorer to see the Oregon Coast. It will never be known for sure.

In compliance with his sovereign mandate, the viceroy dispatched a trio of ships from Acapulco in the spring of 1596 under the command of Sebastian Viscaino. Beyond an attempt to establish two colonies, both of which were unsuccessful because of the so-called sterility of the country, and the savage hostility of the natives, nothing was accomplished. Further activity was delayed following the death of the Spanish king in 1598. But when Philip Ill got the wheels of government going again, he sent direct orders to the viceroy to pursue the survey on up the coast of North America.

It was again to Viscaino that the responsibility fell. This voyage of exploration involved two small caravels and an even smaller "fragata." Viscaino assumed control of the fleet, sailing on the *Captaina* which carried an assortment of men, including pilots, draftsmen and priests so that all discoveries would be properly ascribed in records and with navigation charts.

The voyage was tedious and continued for weeks. It was a wretched band of seafarers that at last gained the portals of San Diego and Monterey. Regrettably, the usual scurvy attacked the crews and many were disabled or perished.

On January 3, 1603, the other two vessels, the *San Diego* and the smaller *Tres Reyes* continued northward. They were separated by a gale and the larger of the two entered a great bay for refuge which may have been San Francisco but more probably Drakes Bay. Here they searched for the remains of the Spanish galleon *San Agustin* wrecked there eight years earlier.

Viscaino resumed his voyage northward until January 20th gaining a point on the Southern Oregon coast, a prominent rocky bluff in Latitude 42 degrees. He applied the name Cape Sebastian. His crew was suffering from scurvy and with the weather threatening, the ship returned to Mexico.

In the approaching gale, the *Tres Reyes* had taken refuge in the lee of Cape Mendocino having become separated from the *Captaina*. When the winds subsided, under pilot Antonio Flores, the vessel sailed northward gaining the 43rd parallel reaching a great headland to which was applied the name Cape Blanco, a landmark which may or may not have been sighted by Ferrelo.

Flores had officially discovered what would one day be known as the most westerly point of Oregon state. At the time, Flores believed that California was an island.

Spain was convinced that little pressing need existed to colonize these unpromising lands whose shores seemed to be swept by gale force winds and pea-soup fogs, or to push on looking for a "northwest passage" near where de Fuca had claimed his strait was located.

Yet, though no official record of de Fuca's discovery was recorded by Spain or Mexico, the approximate location appeared on all navigation charts for the next two centuries. The old Greek's account which appeared in *Purchas, his Pilgrimes,* published in England in 1625, was generally accepted throughout the world.

The headlands of Oregon were becoming familiar to many of those old Spanish shipmasters acting as landfalls to bring them about and set a course southward to Acapulco and San Blas.

Despite the prevailing tales of the mythical strait and of a city of gold called Quivira, the Spanish remembered the stories of hardship and death in the earlier exploits and lost their desire to go north.

By the middle of the 18th century, shocking news of foreign intervention into the neglected lands to the north suddenly made Alta California of great importance to Spain. The Russians had entrenched themselves in Alaska and had, according to rumor, planned to seek real estate to the south. Threatened by possible intervention by the Russians as well as the constant harassment of

English privateers plundering the treasure-laden galleons, Carlos Ill grew determined to build a new stronghold in the Western world to thwart any defying the supremacy of Spain.

By the end of 1768 and early 1769, three ships were launched at the port of San Blas; thus we see a plausible link with ship-wrecks on the Oregon coast.

Father Francis Junipero Sera of the Franciscan order, headed an expedition in 1769 in California "to establish the Catholic religion among numerous heathen peoples. On January 9, 1769, the *San Carlos* sailed from La Paz followed on February 15th by the *San Antonio*.

After losing eight of her crew from scurvy, the *San Antonio* arrived on April 11. Twenty days later, the *San Carlos* managed to limp through the Silver Gate under a few shreds of sail, with only her master, cook and one seaman functioning. All the others had fallen to scurvy. The third vessel, the *San Jose*, never arrived and was listed as missing with all hands. Though generally accepted that she was wrecked somewhere off the Mexican coast, early historians believed this vessel was driven northward by a series of gales suggesting she may have been the second Spanish ship lost in the Nehalem sector of Oregon.

This theory was strongly advanced by historian Silas B. Smith whose mother was Celiast, daughter of Indian Chief Kobaiway of the Clatsops and whose father was Solomon H. Smith. Smith had come overland to Oregon Territory with Nathaniel J. Wyeth in 1832.

Smith believed that the wreck of the *San Jose* represented the second appearance of white man on the Oregon coast. According to the account as revealed to him by the local Nehalems, handed down by their progenitors, a ship carrying men with white skin was driven ashore and wrecked on Nehalem Spit. The crew survived the wreckage and gaining the shore, lived for some time with the natives. A large part of the vessel's cargo was beeswax. The finding of such an abundance of this wax in later years verified the wreck site. In the course of several months, the castaways became obnoxious to their Indian hosts and, according to the narrative, eventually met death. The only memorial to their having been on the Oregon coast is the great amount of beeswax found there.

Other stories of the account vary in detail but the wax was and still is undeniable proof of at least one shipwreck and probably more along that part of Oregon's coastline. Many of the cakes, sized for shipment were ten pounds or more. Some were inscribed with monograms and numerals. One of these bore the letters **I.H.S.** These are the first three letters of the name Jesus, in Greek, and is symbolic of the Roman Catholic faith.

Despite later attempts by mineralogists to pronounce the substance as a paraffin (*ozokerite*) produced in nature, it has now been proven beyond a doubt that it is indeed beeswax and of the Ghedda variety.

Smith was certain that the wreck was the missing *San Jose* which was never again reported after sailing from La Paz on June 16, 1769.

Another persistent story involved the survival of some of the castaways. These men married local Indian women. One of the men was blue-eyed with blonde hair who became the husband of a Nehalem woman, and eventually the father or grandfather of a blue-eyed freckle-faced boy with Indian features. Becoming highly respected, he was part of an Indian family to which belonged a noted chief who resided on the shores of a lake. The chief's name was Cullaby. In Clatsop County, Cullaby Lake today is a popular place.

Edward Cullaby, son of the old chief, told the story to John Ninto in 1845. It involved a supposedly Spanish ship en route from the California missions. Blown off course and wrecked, there remained but one survivor who was found by the Indians.

A young girl named Ona took pity on the castaway and she and her father looked after him while he slowly recovered. The two charitable natives set up shelter near the place where the shipwrecked man had been found because it was a considerable time before he was free enough of pain to accompany them to the tribe's village.

The rescuers were kept in touch with the main camp and Ona learned that the brother of the chief was very angry because the paleface had been saved and he intended to kill him when the opportunity arose.

When the castaway recovered, the chief s brother was very jealous. Ona, on the other hand, had become very fond of him. A skilled and a brave man, he often did better when matched with the Indians in hunting, fishing and in other feats, which only tended to bring more anger against him.

Once, a sudden storm hit an Indian fishing party and destroyed their canoes. All except the chief's brother and one other made it to shore but the castaway managed to rescue them both. Through that act, the chief came to admire him greatly, but the jealous brother, despite the fact his life had been saved, still wanted to kill the "white eyes." He also succeeded in souring other tribal members against the white man.

Becoming close to the chief, the castaway taught him how to use firearms having salvaged some guns and ammunition from the wreck. According to the account, the wreck occurred in the land of the Tillamooks and it was among the Tillamook people the white man lived.

On finding that his daughter was in love with the paleface, and that great animosity was growing among his people, the chief said, "I do not know my own people. We will go to live among the Clatsops. My sister is the wife of their chief."

The lovers were married and the three journeyed north pursued by the jealous chief's son and some of his henchmen. In a showdown, the white man shot his pursuer.

As the story continues, it tells of the castaway and his wife being accepted into the Clatsop tribe and living near a small clay butte on Cullaby Lake with summer dwellings at Neacoxie and Quatat. He instructed the Indians in the use of weapons and became the gunsmith for the tribe.

Then in the late 1700's, just before the turn of the century, after the white man had lived many years among the Clatsops, a ship like the one on which he had been wrecked came near the shore. The crew landed in a small boat but later returned to their ship leaving two of their number behind. Those two soon died of a strange disease which spread among the Tillamooks. Sweeping through the tribe with dire results, the sickness soon reached the Clatsops where hundreds more died.

The white man isolated his family and then went to the

village of Quatat to give what aid he could. Both his father-in-law and the chief's son died and alas, finally the castaway himself.

His and Ona's son, years later, married the daughter of the chief's son. Their offspring was Cullaby or Quaicullaby, for whom the lake is named.

Being an illiterate people, the Indians handed their legends and accounts down by word from one generation to the next. Had only they been able to preserve it in writing, the pages of history would be filled with astounding and dramatic stories. Little doubt remains, however, that early unrecorded shipwrecks, before white man's history was written, occurred on Oregon's beaches, several of them between the mouth of the Columbia River and Tillamook Bay.

A blond Indian is also mentioned in the journals of Lewis and Clark for in their arrival in 1805, sufficient communication with whites had been established to account for such an occurrence without recourse to the event of 1769.

When Lewis & Clark reached the mouth of the Columbia, the Clatsops presented large chunks of beeswax as gifts. The explorers did not know its source.

Captain William Clark wrote in his journal on December 31, 1805:

With the party of Clatsops who visited us last was a man of much lighter colour than the natives are generally. He was freckled with long dusky red hair, about 25 years of age, and certainly must be half white, at least. This man appeared to understand more of the English language than the others of his party but did not speak a word of English. He possesses all the habits of the Indians.

Soto, of whom Gabriel Franchere spoke, was a halfbreed (probably part Indian, part Spanish) found at an Indian village near the Cascade foothills. The nearly blind old man spoke through an interpreter, claiming to be the son of a Spaniard who had been wrecked near the Columbia River. Franchere arrived in Oregon territory in 1811 aboard the ill-fated *Tonquin*. Soto told him:

I was the son of a Spaniard who had been wrecked at the mouth of the river; that a part of the crew on this occasion had got safely ashore, but were all massacred by the Clatsops with the exception of four, who were spared and

51

who married native women; that these four Spaniards of whom his father was one, disgusted with native life, attempted to reach a settlement of their own nation toward the south, but had never been heard from since, and that when his father with his companions, left the country, he himself was quite young.

This further proves the presence of Caucasians among the Indians of Oregon long before recorded discoveries. Alexander Henry of the North West Company at Astoria noted in his journal December 8, 1813:

The old Clatsop chief arrived with some excellent salmon and the meat of a large biche. There came with him a man about 30 years of age who had extraordinary dark red hair, and is the supposed offspring of a ship that was wrecked within a few miles of the entrance of this river many years ago. Great quantities of beeswax continue to be dug out of the sand near this spit, and Indians bring it to trade with us.

On February 28, 1814, the entry in Henry's journal reads:

They bring us frequently lumps of beeswax fresh out of the sand which they collect on the coast to the south where the Spanish ship was cast away some years ago and the crew was all murdered by the Indians.

Fur trader Ross Cox, while at Astoria in 1814, noted that an Indian belonging to a small tribe on the coast, south of the Clatsop country, was fair, his face plainly freckled and his hair red. Slender, and about 5 feet 10 inches tall, Cox described him as of splendid physique, going by the name of Jack Ramsay, a tattoo of sorts on his left arm attesting to that fact. He had not undergone the traditional head flattening practiced by the Oregon coastal Indians but was reputedly the son of an English seafarer who deserted from a trading vessel and took up life among the Indians, taking a squaw as his wife. The elder Englishman had supposedly died in the 1790's. Though he had other children by his Indian wife, only Jack had red hair and virtually none of the Indian features derived from maternal ancestors. To have been survived by a son of Jack's age, the deserter would had to have jumped ship about 1781. During that period, only Cook had sailed along the Oregon coast and he reported no deserters which leaves some questions:

1.. From what English ship could the man in question have come?
2. Was he a pirate?
3. Was he sailing on a vessel other than British?

Missionaries Daniel Lee and Joseph H. Frost, in their book, *Ten Years in Oregon* (see bibliography) wrote:

> ...about 30 or 40 miles to the south of the Columbia are the remains of a vessel which was sunk in the sand near shore, probably from the coast of Asia, laden at least in part with beeswax.

Sol Smith and John Hobson on their 1848 trip along the Oregon Coast between the south entrance of the Columbia River and Nehalem Bay, reported seeing "several pieces of a junk between Clatsop and Nehalem", which Hobson believed to be Chinese. When S. A. Clark, historian, arrived at the scene in the 1870's, he reiterated that there were two wrecks to be seen at the mouth of the Nehalem River.

In 1898, when treasure hunter Pat Smith, one of hundreds who searched for Spanish treasure alleged to be buried on the lower slopes of Mt. Neah-kah-nie or on Nehalem Beach, came upon the remains of a vessel that had been uncovered by shifting sands, he removed several pieces of teak. Efforts by him to get a salvage endeavor underway were thwarted due to lack of funds.

British vice consul E. M. Cherry, when stationed at Astoria, had for many years been intrigued by the promise of Nehalem treasure. He planned a salvage effort to exhume the controversial wreck in 1929, but with the depression and the $30,000 needed for a cofferdam, he could find no investors. Thus the ancient ribs rose and fell with the shifting sands, fluctuating tides and swirling currents.

Though beeswax is still occasionally found along the these beaches, the treasure and the identity of the wrecks has alluded the most dedicated hunters.

Probably no historian of his time researched the maritime mysteries of Nehalem as much as Sol Smith. He relates details of another alleged appearance of white men among the Nehalem Indians which, if true, might have been the first time Caucasians were seen by the Oregon Indians. The legend was told to him from descendants of the tribe:

> Survivors of a shipwreck were seen on an afternoon in strawberry time. The astounded natives watched with fear and trepidation thinking that perhaps their legendary god Tallapus had returned. The ship had been driven on the sands during the night, the first to see the castaways being an Indian woman

from the ocean side of Clatsop Plains. She had wandered down to Clatsop Beach in the early morning and was startled by the appearance of the two strangers with white skin and long flowing beards down to their chests. The wreck from which they had come was lying in the breakers. Just above the driftwood line the survivors had a fire going over which they were cooking some food and popping corn. They made signs to the squaw for 'water.' She in turn, both frightened and excited, ran to the village as fast as her legs would carry her, 'I have found people who are men, and who yet are bears,' she shouted in the midst of the slabboard dwellings.

Leading the tribesmen to the scene, the tribal chief was not fully satisfied that they were really men until he had carefully examined their hands and found they agreed perfectly with his own. They were further amazed by the popping corn, something they had not before seen.

The northern Oregon coastal Indians thereafter referred to all white skinned persons as *Tlo-hon-nipts*, which in translation means, "of those who drift ashore." In other words: "castaways." Apparently those were the first *Tlo-hon-nipts* ever seen by the Indians of northern Oregon. For decades thereafter, they believed that all such people were "those who drift ashore."

The two survivors were soon claimed as slaves. Meanwhile, on learning the value of metal, the Indians recovered all of it from the wreck whenever tide and surf permitted.

When it was discovered that one of the castaways was adept at making knives and tools from iron, the remains of the wreck were burned to obtain every last spike. The Indians named the iron worker, *Konapee*, and though he and his companion were at first made to labor incessantly, in the course of time they were held in high favor and granted the rights of Indian nobility.

Konapee selected a site for his dwelling on the lee side of the Columbia's south entrance, near the historical village seaport of Flavel. This is where the west edge of Young's Bay meets the river. The natives then and long after his death referred to the place as Konapee.*

Among the articles this historic figure had when he was ship-wrecked were numerous Chinese coins. These were retained and became highly cherished by the Clatsop people who referred to the coins as "Konapee's money."

It has often been suggested that the vessel on which Konapee

---

* Konapee is officially listed as a permanent village in *Indians Along the Oregon Trail; the Tribes of Nebraska, Wyoming, Oregon and Washington Identified*. See bibliography.

and his companion came was a Japanese or Chinese junk, which had drifted across the Pacific with the prevailing current system, after becoming disabled at sea. Others claim it to have been a Spanish vessel inasmuch as it was carrying India corn and Chinese cash plus indications that the survivors were evidently Caucasians. This validates claims and other evidence that indeed several prehistoric junks were wrecked on the Pacific Northwest coast.

It is within the realm of possibility that the old Indian to whom Franchere referred as Soto, was the son or grandson of Konapee. Clatsop Indians long claimed that Konapee in later years "reached the land of the sunrise," going from his Clatsop home to the Cascades where he married an Indian woman. Historians have speculated that Konapee may have been ship-wrecked in Oregon about 1725.

If only Konapee could have kept a diary or made contact with the civilized world of his time, he indeed would have held a premier place in the history of Oregon. Very little is known of him except that he was obviously resourceful and intelligent living long among those primitive people gaining both their respect and admiration. Through him, the Clatsop people, and subsequently other tribes, learned about the value of iron for making fishhooks, tools and weapons. In fact, Konapee's knowledge acquired by the Clatsops afforded them prestige and power over rival tribes. Kobaiway, who was chief at the time of the arrival of Lewis and Clark, had acquired all of this knowledge and was considered one of the great chiefs in coast country. He possessed sufficient wealth to support 20 wives and to thus form alliances with other tribes. Many slaves were at his beck and call to take care of the personal wants and the needs of his huge household. Much of his wealth accrued from skills left by Konapee which afforded valuable items for intertribal bartering. Konapee was without a doubt, the first white man to set foot on Oregon real-estate at the mouth of the Columbia River.

Another highly respected Indian leader was the one-eyed Chinook Chief Concomly (sometimes called Comcomly) who resided in a village on the north side of the river entrance near the present town of Chinook.

It is interesting to note that the first white men to visit the Columbia River area, prior to Lewis and Clark, were astounded that the Indians knew the value of iron and that some had metal arrowheads, hatchets and other metal implements. Cook noted the use of iron among the Northwest Indians in 1778 and was of the opinion that it was so widespread that it could not have been introduced by the Spaniards on their voyages of 1774 and 1775. The English explorer further found among the natives considerable copper and brass, "and it is almost a certainty that these come by way of the sea and not by land," observed Cook.

One might ask where all the metal came from that was in the possession of the Indians? The obvious answer is that it was from shipwrecks most likely Spanish, English or Oriental. The Russians, though occupying parts of Alaska in early times, initially had vessels that for the most part were lashed together with leather thongs. The people of Japan could only have made contact with the Indians through castaway junks whose metal supply would at best have been minimal.

What about possible piratical action? The courses and acts of the buccaneers were seldom chronicled. Far more is known of their treachery in the Caribbean and Atlantic than along the Oregon coast, but there was action in the Pacific. John Oxenham, or perhaps the Dutchman Pichilinguies, reaped havoc in the Pacific and though they have not been documented as having been in Pacific Northwest waters, it is not impossible. Sailing countless sea miles, keeping no journals or logs, it is quite plausible that pirates landed in Oregon, buried their treasure and traded metal objects to the Indians for staples and water replenishment. It is further plausible that hostile action against Spanish ships could have resulted off Oregon, one old legend telling of ships firing at each other off Mt. Neah-kah-nie. This naturally leads us to the Treasure Ship story that has become a hallmark of maritime intrigue.

Silas B. Smith whose mother was Celiast, daughter of the Indian chief Kobaiway of the Clatsops, and whose father was Sol Smith, tells of the time-honored legend of a ship

...appearing in the offing at that place [Neah-kah-nie] and coming to, dropped a boat which was rowed ashore. A box, or chest was carried by the

56

men who made a landing and ascended the mountain-side. A hole was then dug, into which was lowered a chest, a black man then being killed, both of which were covered with earth.

The killing of the man is controversial inasmuch as the Indian word for a dead person is similar to that meaning a crucifix. It is also speculation that the chest contained treasure though such tradition has persisted from the outset.

It is a further conjecture that the man killed and buried with the treasure chest was a slave, the pirates aware of the fact that Indians never rifled a grave for fear of spirit retaliation, thus preserving the safety of the chest. Spanish ships frequently took on African slaves available at Manila to any willing to pay the right price. It is also possible that the object thought to be a human form was a cross placed over the chest after it was lowered into the ground. The legend went on to tell of strange figures being cut into several large rocks, supposedly to help find the treasure at a later date or, to mislead any stranger who might try to find its location.

Ever since the arrival of white settlers, those now moss-covered rocks were found with the many strange figures and numerals just as the legend had told and, of course those rocks more than anything else intensified the search. The legend further alleged that the parties that came ashore to bury the treasure chest departed in their ship – the incident being separate from the vessels wrecked on the areas beaches. The reputed location of the chest is on the southwest slope of Neah-kah-nie where through the years the land area became pock-marked with holes dug by seekers. Air holes, ancient drain tiles and hollow spots brought quickened heartbeats but as yet there has been no public claim to finding a single gold doubloon, piece of eight or precious gem. The beaches, on the other hand, have yielded only beeswax and exotic wood.

From time to time an occasional artifact of gold, either of Spanish or oriental origin, was found at various places along the Oregon coast from Cape Perpetua to the Columbia River. This indicates that such treasures fell into Indian hands after the plundering of wrecks.

It is also plausible that the Neah-kah-nie treasure chest, due to the constant erosion, occasional earthquake or seismic activity might have been washed into the sea. Keep in mind, regardless of how much the so-called chest weighed, there is nothing too heavy for the sea to move during the powerful, often devastating winter storms along the Oregon coast. Every indication points to the fact that such an incident did occur. Perhaps long ago and far away some clever soul found a way to purloin the treasure from its well hidden lair and keep his mouth shut. (Not likely!)

Both Hudson's Bay Company and Astor employees were accused at one time or another of secretly removing the treasure for personal gain. But such accusations bore little credence. According to one account, an empty pack train started south from the Astoria trading post in the early 1800's. It went down into Nehalem country and returned with all the packs bulging and each member of the party secretive about the exploit. Rumor persisted the pack train was loaded with loot removed from a place on Neah-kah-nie and, that was how John Jacob Astor (though not present) got started on the road to becoming a millionaire – a wild yarn to be certain!

Now, as to the story of the missing galleon *San Francisco Xavier:* This is reputedly the first vessel wrecked on the Nehalem beach. Built at Cavite in the Philippines in 1691, she measured 175 feet in length with a 50 foot beam. This ship carried 80 cannon and could handle 1,500 tons of cargo. Constructed like other Manila galleons, her frames were of teak and other durable hardwoods. Diocesan records attest to the fact that on one voyage she departed Acapulco with 2,070,000 pesos for trading purposes in the Orient.

The *Xavier* was one of the transpacific galleons that was reported missing at sea in 1705. It has long been conjectured that she is the ship that crashed ashore on Nehalem Beach from which the greater amounts of beeswax found in the area have been extracted. There is considerable evidence to allow for the claim,

> ...unknown waves before
> me roll, hiding rocks
> and treacherous shoal.
> —an hymn "Jesus, Savior Pilot Me"

much of which has already been presented in the Indian legends of shipwreck and of the traces of Caucasian blood found among the early Indians. It is also quite plausible that in addition to her bees-wax cargo, the galleon carried treasure inasmuch as she disappeared while returning to the West Coast from the Indies.

> **The Mystery Crucifix**
> In recent years, an amateur diver visited the author and proudly displayed a small silver crucifix he said he found while diving off Nehalem beach. Although this artifact bore no identification, it might plausibly be from the old Spanish wreck.

Adding to the complexities of the tangled riddles of shipwreck in early Oregon, is another intriguing incident that centers around Three Rocks, near the mouth of the Salmon River. This is 23 miles north of Yaquina Head. Lying about 800 yards offshore, the three grayish outcrops have become symbolic with an ancient shipwreck which reputedly occurred between there and the river mouth. Referred to as Three Rocks wreck, the persistent legend somewhat parallels those of Mt. Neah-kah-nie and the Nehalem beaches.

In the depths of the past, Indians told the first white settlers in the Cascade Head area (the Salmon River empties into the ocean at the southern extremity of Cascade Head) of a white-winged ship that years before had been wrecked at the mouth of the Salmon River. Strange men came ashore and buried a treasure chest.

The story was received somewhat with tongue-in-cheek until years later when pieces of wreckage were found on the beach. Fishermen further complained of snagging their nets on some underwater obstruction off the river entrance. In 1931, while clearing a summer camping site for tourists, E. G. Calkins, owner of the land (a former County Commissioner) at Three Rocks Beach, came upon a mysterious find. The area had been in-habited by Indians for hundreds of years before any white men arrived and there were many mounds full of shells and middens. While leveling a mound with his plowshare, Calkins came across some Indian relics. Interested friends came with rakes and hoes to carefully search. They found such items as whalebone war clubs, stone pestles and a broken iron kettle – not unusual instruments for old Indian camp sites. Nearby, however, was unearthed an oversized human thigh bone which aroused considerable interest. Further probing of the soil produced the entire skeletal remains of a "giant." Its skull was two-thirds of an inch thick with broad cheekbones and forehead and a perfect set of large teeth. Nearby, a normal sized skeleton was uncovered. Obviously, this "superman" was the center of attention.

Dr. F. M. Carter, physician, and Oregon historian Dr. John Horner were called in to give their expert opinions of the find. Carter, after his examination, was astounded to discover what had once been an eight foot giant of the Negro race. Some of his huge bones were cracked or broken suggesting he might have been tortured before death came. The skull of the smaller skeleton, reputedly Caucasian, appeared to have been pierced by an arrow or struck by some weighty instrument.

Calkins and his neighbors reasoned the find to be evidence of ancient pirate activity and began to look for clues to the treasure so long rumored to have been buried in the area. As a direct link, they turned their attention toward the ancient wreck said to be lying off the Salmon River. Those who had encountered the obstruction claimed it was perhaps 100 to 150 feet in length. Calkins and others before him had occasionally recovered pieces of hardwood ribs with copper bolts in them.

Long before the skeletal finds, Dr. Carter was familiar with the long standing legend of the Three Rocks wreck, and a persistent tale of 20 men who reputedly buried a chest leaving two of their number to guard the spot, while the rest moved on. One was said to have been a large black man who later quarreled with and struck dead his companion, a white man. The Negro then incurred the wrath of the local Indians who turned upon him and killed him.

As early as 1603, Morga, a governor of the Philippines, visited Mexico and told of his islands supplying New Spain (Mexico) with gold, cotton, cloth, *mendrinaque* (general cargo) and cakes of white and yellow wax. The year of Morga's visit was near the same period that an earlier galleon had disappeared with all hands probably somewhere along the West Coast. If not in California waters, perhaps it was in Oregon. The location where the ship was lost has never been established.

In the summer of 1974, Edward Calkins, son of the late Elmer G. Calkins, on whose land the skeletal remains were discovered in 1931, applied to the U. S. Army Corps of Engineers for a permit to dredge in a tide flat at the entrance to the Salmon River. He wanted to exhume the ancient remains of what has been referred to as the Three Rocks wreck. Plans were to dredge an area 30 feet wide, 70 feet long and ten feet deep using a land-based crane with a clamshell and dragline bucket. An exploratory hole was to be dug first to ascertain that the obstruction was actually a wrecked ship. Hoping to find items of great value within, and to link the wreck with the skeletal remains found nearby years earlier, Calkins pursued his desire with the encouragement of historians and many other interested parties.

The story related to him by his father was virtually the same as the aforementioned, both originating from Indian legend:

A monstrous canoe with wings was blown into the mouth of the Salmon River and wrecked. This version, however, mentions three men instead of two – a giant black and two Caucasian companions having been left to guard something of value recovered from the wreck, supposedly a chest or box containing treasure. Twenty others left the scene to make their way south to New Spain, but were never heard from again.

The three who remained lived among the Indians for a considerable time. The Negro, because of his great stature and strength was being worshipped as a god.

When his mortality was proven, the Indians became angered with the strangers and in a skirmish, all three were murdered.

Alas— Calkins had his request for dredging revoked by both the Army Engineers and the State of Oregon where the reason was the possible damage to estuary life. The 60 year old Lake Oswego man was further informed that there was "insufficient evidence of shipwreck in or near the Salmon River area."

Calkins presented several reasons for believing the wreck to be in the Salmon River estuary. He exhibited some news photographs taken in 1931 of the burial site where the skeletal remains were uncovered by his father while he was leveling ground for his campsite at the Three Rocks resort community on the north bank of the river. The ancient Indian midden gave mute evidence of the three strangers sharing a violent death. One of the leg bones was shown to have been shattered. There was a two-inch bone spearhead lodged at the base of one skull. There was a

Photograph from microfilm of *Oregon Sunday Journal* issue of Sunday, April 26, 1931 page 3. This was a major feature story and attracted wide attention because of the credibility of the participants. Legend under picture is from the microfilm.

Skull of ancient Indian, found in a shell mound at the mouth of Salmon river in Lincoln county, showing a bone arrow 2 inches long which had just been extracted from base of the skull by Dr. John B. Horner of the Oregon State college historian. Center, above, Dr. F. M. Carter, who for many years has practiced medicine among the Indians, holding one of the Indian skulls; G. F. Calkins who uncovered the mound containing the skeleton that may have once belonged to the giant Negro pirate.

The editor specifically recalls viewing a cardboard box of skulls and bones in the Horner Museum in 1974. The single staff person said these were "Indian," were unidentified and questioned keeping them.

large stone imbedded in another. It appeared as though the trio had been set upon with a vengeance by a large number of natives.

The late professor Dr. John B. Horner, who had been earlier asked to express his views on the skeletal find in 1931, was an historian at Oregon State College (now University) and an expert on Indian lore. It was he who gathered up all the contents of the shell mound and midden and took them to Corvallis for a museum which was then in the planning stages on the campus. His studies showed the bone remains to be from 260 to 300 years old which would have dated the incident prior to the mid 1600's. His estimates were partially made from the size of the spruce trees that Calkins cleared from atop the burial site. Witnesses claimed the diameter of the trees to be as "large as table tops."

It was not till 1973 that the latter Calkins revived his interest in the Tree Rocks wreck attempting to prove his father's theory of a link between the wreck and the grave site. Then the plot thickened. He went to Oregon State University to research the items removed from the grave site years earlier. He found nothing. No bones. No skulls. No artifacts. In fact, even the 3,000 word essay Horner had written on the historical find was missing. Apparently nobody at the university could or would shed any light on the subject.

Perhaps it was a story that appeared in a Portland newspaper, the *Oregon Journal* on April 26, 1931, that prompted many amateur and professional treasure seekers to search the Salmon River area. Was this disappearance of the material caused by some misguided latter-day pirate seeking to get the inside track — or was it a housekeeping matter at the Horner Museum?

Skeptics who saw the artifacts removed from the site claimed them not to be Indian in nature. The so-labeled war club was, they claim, the remains of a belaying pin. The stone pestle was a ballast rock. A teapot or kettle originated from a foreign country. All of this appears to reject the theory of violence. One way or the other, the strangers in the grave were other than Indian and they had been there long before the recorded coming of the white man to the Oregon coast.

Dooming Calkins' recovery of the wreck was legislation enacted in 1975 proclaiming 9,670 acres of land surrounding Cascade Head to be a federally protected scenic and scientific research area – including the Salmon River estuary. The State of Oregon claims it the "smallest and most pristine on the Oregon Coast." Is the matter closed? The State Land Board was impressed with Calkins' request and did not rule out the plausibility of some future scientific follow up.

Calkins recalled that his father had told him of gillnetting at the mouth of the Salmon River as early as 1913. On several occasions his nets had become tangled on an obstruction seven or eight feet below the surface within 300 yards of the place where the skeletons were unearthed 18 years later. Twice when his nets were pulled free, bits of wreckage, including a curved piece of wood resembling the rib of a ship, were attached. Among the items discovered were heavily corroded copper nails. Other gill-netters also complained of the obstruction which at that time was considered some worthless hulk.

Calkins believed that this same hulk may have been the legendary Spanish treasure ship.

A metal detector has been used in the area and has shown definite activity in one particular spot near where the wreck is alleged to be. A 14 foot steel probe has outlined a submerged wooden object at about the nine foot depth. Two woodworking experts have suggested half-inch core samples taken from the sunken object show a variety of ironwood originating only in the Southern Hemisphere.

With all the intrigue involved concerning possible recovery of this mysterious ship, the State has stood fast on its conclusions that it wants to keep the Salmon River Estuary intact. But it leaves the door open for a future dig.

On one hand we see a potential opportunity to add to the historical background of our coast area and on the other hand we see the proposed disturbance of a fragile estuarine area of great value.... The division is charged to protect the aquatic resources of the waters of this state. However, everyone benefits from new information on historical events. We are not prepared to close the door on a possible historical or treasure trove find... The Division of State Lands would consider a subsequent application in this matter, provided that additional substantive evidence of the ship is obtained by non-destructive testing and submitted to the division.

Will the real answer ever be known?

Another intriguing find of ancient vintage on the Oregon coast was a 20-foot copper-sheathed beam discovered at Del Rey Beach, north of Gearhart by Clatsop County Commissioner Dave Megrath in the winter of 1973. The nails holding the copper to the wood were all stamped with the traditional "broad arrow" insignia used by the British Admiralty since 1661. This was to mark naval stores. The beam now at the Columbia River Maritime Museum in Astoria could have come from the *HMS Sulphur*, wrecked in 1839 on Clatsop Spit off the Columbia River bar. Or it may have come from some unrecorded wreck of an earlier British ship or privateer.

Michael Naab, former curator at the museum, said records show copper sheathing was not introduced on Admiralty ships until 1771. The broad arrow insignia was also found stamped in double rows on the drift pins protruding from the sides of the beam.

Indian legend told of another ancient vessel being wrecked near the mouth of Elk Creek near Cannon Beach. Some of the remains were later seen by the pioneers. Part of the wreckage of the *USS Shark,* wrecked on Clatsop Spit in 1846, also drifted ashore south of Cannon Beach, a cannon affixed to the piece of decking being responsible for the naming of the town. The rusted old weapon and the ship's capstan are displayed in the museum of the Clatsop County Historical Society on Exchange Street in Astoria.

The late Senator Richard Neuberger of Oregon, an historian in his own right, believed the remains of the giant black man unearthed near Salmon River was interrelated with the incident at Nehalem. According to his speculative conclusions, the Negro was the slave of his Caucasian companions. They were survivors of the wreck and were responsible for the removal and burying of the fabled chest. It was fact that blacks from East Africa, as we read earlier, were commonly used as slaves. They were publicly sold in places like Manila and it was common practice on the galleons to allow passengers to bring their slaves as attendants on Pacific crossings. Neuberger's theory was that the men buried the chest well above the tide line below Mt. Neah-kah-nie then, being castaways from the nearby wreck, began their trek southward. On reaching the Salmon River they encountered hostile Indians where they were set upon and murdered.

If the wreck, or one of the wrecks, of ancient vintage lying off Nehalem beaches is the *San Francisco Xavier,* there could be a fortune in gold, silver or gems awaiting the finder. If one of the wrecks in the Columbia River, Nehalem or Salmon River areas is the *San Antonio,* (rumored to have been wrecked near San Miguel Island west of Los Angeles), the treasure could be even more alluring. As she was about to sail from Manila in 1603, the Chinese and Filipinos were engaged in a massive revolt. With her destination as Acapulco, the ship became the sanctuary of several wealthy families of influential Spanish officials who sought safety and protection in New Spain. With them went fabulous amounts of personal treasure – millions of dollars in uncut stones, jewelry, cash, gold and silver bullion in addition to the general cargo carried by every galleon. It is claimed that the vessel departed Manila with more riches than any other galleon in the two and a half centuries of Pacific trade. It is not impossible that the ship, which disappeared without trace, lies wasting away off the Oregon coast and not in California waters as some have suspected. While speculation is intriguing, the truth may never be known.

These and the other early Spanish wrecks which occurred along the Oregon and Washington coasts in the 17th and 18th centuries, indicate far more early activity by Caucasian mariners in Pacific Northwest waters than history has recorded.

Some historians have speculated that Spanish explorers visited and examined what we know today as the Curry County coast of Oregon, then sailed northward, entered the Umpqua River where they refitted. This conjecture has no official source.

Toward the end of the 18th century, Spain dispatched the *San Carlos* from Mexico to find out whether San Francisco Bay could be entered from the ocean side. In June 1775, the small caravel passed safely through the Golden Gate and dropped her hook. This action caused more uneasiness on the part of England, because of her arch enemy's influence and her empire-growing in North America.

New agitation and threats of war were rampant. Spanish ships next sailed as far north as British Columbia gaining a firm foothold at Nootka Sound and endeavoring to set up a fortress at Neah Bay inside the entrance to the Strait of Juan de Fuca. Sub-Lieutenant Manual Quimper brought the *Princesa Real* to the latter destination in 1791 but the little brick fortress was unsuccessful and soon fell into decay.

Three years earlier, Estevan Martinez, ex-pilot of Juan Perez, commanding the *Princesa,* and Lieutenant Gonzalo Haro, in the *San Carlos*, explored many of the islands, inlets and straits on the lee side of Vancouver Island. Retaliation from England almost touched off a major war between the two maritime nations.

When Captain Robert Gray sailed along the Oregon coast and officially discovered Tillamook Bay in 1788, the question remained as to whether he was actually the first Caucasian seen by the Tillamook Indians or, the first white explorer to land in Oregon. Items his men found in the possession of the Indians gave every indication of early contact with castaways, or perhaps visiting pirates.

Along the shores of Yaquina Bay, skeletal remains of Caucasians were discovered many years ago and nearby were found several copper coins bearing the inscription, "English Trade Tokens 1788." There was also a brass handled ship's cutlass.

Bancroft, in his *History of the Northwest Coast,* wrote:

In 1700-1750, the Philippine treasure ships continued to cross the Pacific by the northern route without touching on the California coast and a French vessel under Fondac took the same course.

The sea-roving adventurers of other centuries who came from the old world, pitting their frail ships against the unknown tempest, may well have dropped anchor at one or more of the indentations along the Oregon coast for refuge from storms or for replenishment of water.

Perhaps the discovery of Oregon belongs to the Spanish navigator Bartolme Ferrelo who, sailing north of California as earlier told, entered the latitude of Oregon in 1543. As will be recalled, he served as Cabrillo's pilot in 1542-1543, but when Cabrillo died, his final instructions were to sail northward. He reputedly reached Cape Blanco then was forced to retreat before adverse weather, sickness and because rations had been reduced to a few biscuits.

Stories of Spanish treasure and shipwreck have crept into every area along the Oregon coast, but perhaps the center of the most lore and intrigue continues to center around Mt. Neah-kah-nie and the Nehalem beaches. At Treasure Cove, on the northern base of Neah-kah-nie, is a cave just above the tide line, the name having derived from tales of pirate treasure legends told by the Indians. According to the legend, three strange vessels engaged in a battle offshore in ancient times.

North of Treasure Cove is Smugglers Cove with just its name offering piratical overtones. These two places have also beckoned many adventurous treasure seekers.

Commercial fishermen from Garibaldi long claimed that a vessel had been sighted in the depths near Neah-kah-nie's Short Sands Beach and was believed to be of Spanish origin.

Further south, pirate treasure has long been rumored near the Rogue River entrance.

Gold bullion is alleged to have been found by divers off the entrance to the Columbia River presumed from the bowels of an ancient ship. And other little treasures have been uncovered along the coast through the years. The finders usually keep their troves a secret for fear of others invading the site and of Uncle Sam slapping a healthy tax on their finds.

It would be safe to say that both Orientals and Caucasians dwelled among the coastal Indians for centuries but the mists of time have secreted their activities forever. Still more evidence remains to be found, and who knows, maybe some day a lucky beachcomber will discover a vast treasure. ☐

Mouth of Winchuck River is at Winchuck State Wayside on the south Oregon coast – way south only a few *feet* north of California.

Chapter 5
Junks Along the Northwest Coast

> **Who Reached Oregon First?**
> It would be this writer's hypothesis
> that the shores of Oregon were known
> to many foreigners long before record-
> ed discoveries and that some of these
> strangers were Orientals.

Try this for size:

It is alleged and preserved through Indian legend that about 500 years ago, just before Columbus discovered America, an old Chinaman survived the wreck of his junk on the shores of Oregon. Turning pirate, he enlisted a host of blood-thirsty savages, (bad Indians) who, using war canoes, ranged between the Columbia River and Coos Bay – even as far south as the Coquille River pillaging and plundering one native village after another. The fierce Oriental taught his redskin buccaneers how to make and wield weapons of metal which were used with frightening results on their victims.

Such a legend is by no means preposterous for it is a fact that more than 60 Oriental junks were found wrecked or adrift in the Pacific Ocean up till 1876.* Before such information was

---

* The most recently discovered junk was the Japanese *Ryo Yei Maru* out of Misaka, which was discovered 15 miles south of the Umatilla Reef Lightship on October 31, 1927. The drifting hulk was spotted by a lookout on the *SS Margaret Dollar* (Captain H. T. Payne). It was towed to Seattle. Documents found on board indicated the fishing junk sailed from Misaka on December 5, 1926. On December 12th the crank-shaft broke. Due to stiff winds, the sail could not be hoisted and the junk drifted out of control. On December 26th the vessel entered the North Pacific Drift current and "heading east for America. No compass to guide." On May 10th was the last entry. The *Ryo Yei Maru* drifted for nearly six more months before being sighted by the *Margaret Dollar*. Of 12 who had been on board, all died. Alas, the translation of the ship's name is "Good and Prosperous." Data from *Wrecked Japanese Junks Adrift in the North Pacific Ocean.* See bibliography.   —bw

available, hundreds, maybe thousands of junks were blown away from the forbidden land of the rising sun by stress of weather or breakdowns, drifting with the prevailing currents toward the North American continent. The plausibility exists some of these could have been Chinese. Horace Davis (1872) and Charles W. Brooks (1875) established that the evidence is most convincing that the vast majority of all junks adrift in the open ocean were Japanese. In the year 1874 alone, some 22,000 junks were registered in Japan and many were found derelict or wrecked from Alaska to Mexico, in the Hawaiian Islands and some even in the South Seas.

One is known to have been wrecked on Clatsop Beach, just south of the Columbia River in 1820, and five years before that another came ashore near Point Conception, California. Still another was cast ashore near Cape Flattery, Washington in 1833.* A junk is believed to have been wrecked on the island of Maui in Hawaii as early as the 13th century. Nobody knows how many of these ancient craft were rudely deposited on Northwest shores before recorded history.

Japan was an empire as early as 660 B.C., under Emperor Jimmu, proverbial descendant of the sun goddess. Even if one measures that nation by the foundation of the Japanese state, laid in the 5th century by the Yamato clan, whose chief priest assumed the role of emperor, it is ancient. Japan borrowed heavily on Chinese culture in the 6th and 8th centuries and its modes of water transport, exclusively by junk, modified from the Chinese version, varied to some extent through the years. It is only natural to assume that scores of these craft were swept away from the home shores. Japan was a closed nation and by strict edict, its people were forbidden from departing in vessels that could survive a transpacific crossing, on warning of death. During the Edict Period of Japanese history (1636-1853), junks were re-

---

* The junk that stranded near Cape Flattery had three survivors. After being rescued by Indians, and made slaves, they were rescued by Dr. John McLoughlin of the Hudson's Bay Company. When these "waifs" (survivors) finally reached Fort Vancouver, they were put in the settlement's school. Not only was the fact that these waifs survived the transpacific drift in an open boat unique, other uniquenesses are that it was an American missionary school teacher from Oregon who taught these Japanese adult students in a British School in what became the State of Washington. For the complete story refer to *Dr. John McLoughlin, Master of Fort Vancouver, Father of Oregon.* See bibliography.

Sketch of typical Japanese junk of the post-Edict period.

designed in such a way that their self-destruction would be guaranteed when caught in storms in the open ocean. It was some of these junks that drifted, uncontrollable, to North America. Strangers were likewise forbidden to enter Japan for if they did, they faced execution.

China's history antedates that of Japan. Hsia is traditionally called the first dynasty, but Shang (1523-1027 B.C.) is the first in documented history. Chinese junks, for centuries the most seaworthy vessels afloat, were unexcelled in junkdom and far better designed and constructed than their Japanese and Formosan counterparts.

Not only capable of crossing the Pacific under sail, they could further remain seaworthy in any ocean and against the most storm-tossed seas. However, the early Chinese showed little inclination toward eastward crossings of the Pacific, preferring the better known trade routes along the Asian and African continents.

Marco Polo once recited the wonders of the junk, claiming it to be the finest craft afloat. First to have watertight compartments, balanced rudders and battened sails, such vessels were honored for lengthy voyages in ancient times. Still on the scene in

71

China in the nuclear age, junks were perhaps the finest deep-water vessels until the advent of modern shipbuilding technology. Registered up to 400 tons, some junks carried 200 to 300 persons. Fashioned with two or more layers of planks and three to five masts, they had as many as 50 separate cabins for merchants, passengers and crew.

It has been stated the junk may have had its origin in China more than 4,800 years ago and developed gradually into a highly seaworthy, and somewhat complex vessel, despite its rather unorthodox exterior appearance.

With such efficient ships, the Chinese mastered the rudiments of fishing and trading along the country's vast coastline. They also became a great naval power in the 1500's under the Ming Dynasty, boasting 3,100 war junks, 400 transports, and 250 multi-masted treasure ships, claimed to have been up to 300 feet in length with beams of 150 feet.

Chinese tradition tells of a junk that set out from China in 219 B.C., its destination, the "Isle of the Blest." That destination may be what we know today as Japan, but unfortunately the junk was driven eastward for months by a series of terrible gales to a mysterious foreign land called Fu-sang, possibly the Oregon or California coast.

There was a similarity with some Oriental words among the early dialects of Northwest Indians, and the fusion of Oriental characteristics in physical features indicated intercourse between the two races. It is a near certainty that Japanese or Chinese people viewed the shore of Oregon long, long before sightings by Spanish eyes or those of other foreigners. They, however, probably came not by choice but by accident, being driven from their Oriental habitats by the undeniable forces of nature, many never again to return from whence they had come. □

Chapter 6
Indian Encounters

Fact: All of America once belonged to the Indians
Fact: White man purloined it from the natives

Illiterate, satisfied and shunning progress, the red man was ripe for exploitation and the cruel process nearly led to his extermination. Those who fought back were considered savages of the most despicable kind. Often mistreated and detested, their acts of reprisal were sometimes bloodthirsty. But such ways were, to the defiant ones, the only apparent way to seek revenge.

Any white who sympathized or took the side of the Indian was ridiculed.*

Few were the friends of the exploited, possible exceptions being the clergy and Indian agents, who often fought a losing battle in gaining justified rights for the conquered.

Despite the attitude toward the "true" Americans, many befriended the white settler offering invaluable assistance in time of need. This was often without thanks or any compensation.

Though many skirmishes erupted between the hostile Indians and the early white settlers in the southern half of Oregon territory, northerly tribes along the coast were a far more peaceful and, generally speaking, presented little resistance to the white man's government which eventually relegated them to reservations.

The Rogue River War of 1855-56 was the most significant

---

*When a man in Jacksonville, Oregon made public speeches about leaving the Indians alone, he was threatened with tar and feathers. He successfully escaped in the nick of time in the middle of the night. The story is in *John Beeson's Plea For the Indians; His Lone Cry in the Wilderness for Indian Rights – Oregon's First Civil-Rights Advocate.* See the bibliography.

Indian uprising in Oregon. The most important of the many forts constructed to throttle the Indian belligerents was Fort Lane in Jackson County named for the first governor of Oregon territory.

Just how long the Indians had resided on the Oregon coast before the coming of the white man is an unsolved question. Ethnologist John P. Harrington once stated:

> Indian ownership of the coast reached back doubtless for a hundred generations. A map in 500 A.D. probably would have shown the same ownership as that made by Lewis and Clark 1,300 years later.

Some ethnologists believe these people originally migrated across the top of the world where Siberia and Alaska now almost touch. Some carbon datings of artifacts at Lake Takenitch, south of Florence suggest this is true. This compares with the white man's fraction of ownership of less than two centuries. Though the coastal Indians left no monuments, no buildings and only a simple culture, they used the land with the wisest of conservation methods and did little to mark it with ruin. In fact, in all of the hundreds of years the Indians owned Oregon, it remained, for the most part, just the way they found it and God made it. In less than two centuries, white man's civilization, with its so-called progress, has destroyed much of its natural beauty and is now in a desperate battle to save what remains.

Though the Oregon coast is still beautiful, some of its original charm has faded like the last rose of summer.

When Lewis and Clark came west they found the sizes of the Oregon coast tribes varied greatly in number. They estimated the Coos (also called "Hanis Coos") population at 1,500. (In 1910 there were only 93. By 1930 the U.S. Census reported 197. The Office of Indian Affairs in 1937 recorded 55.)*

Some of the tribes were even larger. But by the middle 1850's, some had almost been eliminated as the Port Orfords, the smallest, with only 27 total: nine men, nine women and nine children.

The chief's name was as big as his tribe: Chat-al-hak-e-ah.

The Port Orford area, an ancient coastal Indian stamping ground, was the scene of an historic struggle between the Indians

* *Indians Along the Oregon Trail*...p. 74. See bibliography.

Battle Rock at Port Orford, was scene of serious battle between hundreds of Indians and nine whites in 1851.

and would-be settlers. The year was 1851.

Captain William Tichenor, one of the earliest to navigate the Pacific Coast by steam powered vessel, played a major role in the incident. That experienced mariner was the skipper-owner of the steamer *Sea Gull*. He hauled freight and a few passengers between San Francisco and the Columbia River. With an eye toward creating a settlement on a prosperous appearing location from where trade could be carried on by sea, he was intrigued by the Port Orford area. He visualized a town built on the half-moon-shaped bay. As there were many mining ventures in the mountains, he envisioned having his new town become the port facility to serve these businesses.

Tichenor took his steamer to the then pioneer town of Portland and there talked up the merits of his project. The captain's enthusiasm found attentive ears and soon a party of nine eager participants were loading their gear aboard the *Sea Gull*. Taken aboard aside from provisions were firearms, a small cannon and appropriate tools.

Sailing southward, after a stop at Astoria for extra arms, the steamer landed the men at Port Orford on the morning of June 9, 1851. The colonizers were John M. Kirkpatrick, J. H. Egan, Joseph Hussey, Cyrus W. Hedden, R. Erastus "Jake" Summers,

T. D. Palmer, George Ridoubt, John T. Slater all men in good health and ready for a rugged adventure.

While the initial efforts were underway, Captain Tichenor joined the landing party long enough to help survey the area, then bidding the men farewell departed for San Francisco to purchase additional supplies saying he would return shortly.

While the unloading was going on, Indians watched with curiosity. Once the *Sea Gull* left, they became troublesome and abusive. The settlers suddenly found themselves in dire straits. Fearing for their lives, they quietly worked their way to a prominent bastion just a broad-jump from the beach – a place that was destined to become known as Battle Rock. With great effort, the nine moved their provisions up the steep slope of the rock and set up the cannon and prepared to defend themselves. They didn't have a long wait. The next day the Indians returned but now they brought friends which swelled their ranks.

Shortly after dawn, the attack began and the battle was on with a hail of arrows. With vastly superior numbers, the redmen moved up the hill. With the only access full of Indians, there was no escape other than to jump off the rock into the sea below. The

Low tide winter breakers due west of Best Western Motel in Gold Beach.

leader of the white brigade, Kirkpatrick, in desperation touched off the little cannon which when fired "caused a vacancy in the crowd." This was followed by fire from the rifles, some of the retreating Indians falling in their tracks.

Counter-attacking natives broke into the camp but were promptly knocked down with gun butts even though two of the white men were wounded. Palmer was shot in the neck and Redoubt had an arrow sticking into his breast bone. For 15 minutes musket fire and arrows passed each other in flight, but the superior firepower finally forced the Indians to break ranks and retreat leaving a dozen of their number dead.

The settlers knew it was but a matter of time until the Indians would resume the battle, and if not annihilated the settlers would be starved out. Further, their supply of ammunition was fast dwindling.

While the Indians were holding a war dance on the beach, Kirkpatrick and the others, silently slipped off the rock and headed into the woods and to ultimate safety.*

Years later, Tichenor distinguished himself (1869) by taking the first shipload of lumber across the tricky Coquille bar for the account of Grube, Pohl & Rink who had established a sawmill on the north side of the river above Parkersburg.

Several other incursions by hostile Indians erupted on Oregon's southern coast where the coming of the white man was firmly protested.

After Captain Levi Scott laid plans for the town of Scottsburg on the Umpqua, in 1850, Winchester, Payne & Co. dispatched the schooner *Samuel Roberts,* Captain Coffin, up the coast from California with supplies. On the way, two other rivers were mistaken for the Umpqua. The schooner first tried to enter the Klamath River (in California) and found it unnavigable. Next, it was the Rogue River where two of the company's crew rowed ashore and were promptly surrounded by a band of abusive Indians. Poking at and taunting the intruders, the Rogue tribesmen ripped the buttons from the whitemen's clothing. Tempers flared and the entrapped men retaliated by shoving the Indians away

---

* For the full account, with pictures, refer to: *Battle Rock, the Hero's Story; A True Account–Oregon Coast Indian Attack...* See bibliography.

with their gun butts, not daring to fire for fear of their lives.

Captain Coffin, observing their predicament, worked the schooner close to shore where he fired a cannon charge of nails and grapeshot which landed in the trees over the heads of the Indians. Terrified, with the leaves quivering above their heads, they fled into the forest. Quickly seizing this chance to escape, the two whites launched their skiff and made a hasty retreat to the schooner.

The northerly voyage continued until the ship reached the Umpqua River where the *Samuel Roberts* successfully crossed the bar. It was perhaps the first commercial deep sea vessel to enter the river.

Word spread concerning the potential of the Umpqua area with its tall stands of timber and adequate bar entrance, plus the fact that the Indians were not as troublesome as those to the south.

Winchester, Payne & Co. fitted out the schooner *Kate Heath* which came north from San Francisco with 100 men. Among them was A. C. Gibbs who was elected Governor of Oregon in 1862.

As the *Heath* entered the river on Oct. 10, 1850, a wrecked ship was seen hard on the shoals at the entrance which greatly surprised the pioneer party. She was the *Bostonian* which had been dispatched around the Horn from Boston under Captain Woods for the account of a merchant named Gardiner. While attempting to cross the bar, the vessel had missed stays, drifted out of the main channel and became firmly implanted on the sands. Efforts to refloat the ship failed and the supercargo (the business manager aboard), George Snelling, Gardiner's nephew, directed the unloading of the cargo. This freight was taken upriver a few miles and sheltered beneath a canvas covering of salvaged sails. This place was named Gardiner and is so known to this day.

The Umpqua bar was destined to achieve a sinister reputation. Though pioneer shipmaster Captain J. B. Leeds rendered an opinion that it was the least dangerous on the Oregon coast, the later factors determined his was not the best conclusion. The larger percentage of the initial ocean-going vessels to cross the bar came to grief but none of these were due to Indian hostility:

Bostonian,	October 1, 1850
Caleb Curtis	1851
Almira	January, 9, 1852
Nassau	July 22, 1852
Roanoke	February 2, 1853
Oregon	1854
Loo Choo	1855

Old town Waldport is actually built over an Indian burial ground. When the town was platted, the remains of scores of dead and their decaying canoes were piled together and burned without the slightest thought of reburial. Anything of value was removed from the canoe caskets and kept for personal gain.

So often the white man labeled the Indian as a savage, a vermin of sorts that needed to be stamped out. Those American natives were considered a thorn in the side if they stood in the way of "progress."

Frances Fuller Victor records the details of an epidemic that was passed to the Clatsop Indians after an early ship visited the area. The sickness spread down the coast from one tribe to the next eventually taking with it the lives of thousands of Indians. This was only one of several such incidents. Many other natives became victims of "firewater," – becoming hopeless alcoholics. There was the tragic spread of venereal disease transmitted from the Caucasian. Sometimes entire tribes were found to be infected.

David Douglas, the British botanist, on visiting the Clatsop country, recorded in his journal on October 11, 1830:

A dreadfully fatal intermittent fever broke out in the lower parts of this [Columbia] river about eleven weeks ago, which had depopulated the country. Villages which had afforded from one to two hundred effective warriors are totally gone; not a soul remains. The houses are empty and flocks of famished dogs are howling about, while dead bodies lie strewn in every direction on the sand of the river.*

Chief Kilchis, one of the finest and most respected of the Tillamook tribe, a man who often befriended the white settlers, was a typical victim of outright disrespect. It was he who showed the first white settler to come to his land, Joe Champion, in 1851,

---

* For more about David Douglas as well as about this fatal malady that caused so much death to the Indians, refer to *Dr. John McLoughlin, Master of Fort Vancouver, Father of Oregon.* See bibliography.

where he could find shelter and a temporary home in the massive stump of a hollow spruce tree. He told his people:

> I do not like to see the white man come to Tillamook because wherever he goes he takes all the land, but there is nothing we can do about it, so, it is best not to hurt his feelings.

Fighting blood was far more apparent in the Indians of Southern Oregon and the difficulties with the Coquille and Rogue River Indians in the 1850's increased almost daily. Making no attempt to hide their objections to the white invasion, they were ready and willing to resist the trespass upon their lands. But their best efforts were little more than a holding action against superior forces. Lt. Colonel Silas Casey was sent from San Francisco, under orders from General Hitchcock, with an army of 90 soldiers, to set up a fort at Port Orford for the express purpose of punishing the Coquilles for any hostile acts.

By 1852, prospectors had moved into many parts of Southwest Oregon, including the vicinity around Ellensburg (Gold Beach). On the coast, there was gold* to be panned from the beach sands. This activity rallied the Indians to try to protect their interests with acts of hostility. The pioneers were always quick to respond, usually with even greater violence.

Robbing Indian graves was a pastime of many early settlers. Even in death the Indians could not rest in peace. □

---

* Refer to *Gold Mining in Oregon*. See bibliography.

Chapter 7
Heroes and Cowards in the Surf

About a century ago when a ship was aground on the Oregon coast, oar-propelled surf boats were the principal tool in rescue operations. Often pulled by teams of steaming horses to the wreck location, the boats were either manned by volunteer crews or the trained personnel of the United States Lifesaving Service.

These crews of men in remarkable boats were responsible for saving scores of lives. The Lifesaving Service, operating on all of the coasts of the nation was made up of strong, hard-working men. The Oregon coast had several stations. These were located at:

Cape Disappointment
Hammond
Tillamook Bay
Yaquina Bay
Umpqua River
Coos Bay (at Cape Arago)

Precursor to the present day Coast Guard search and rescue operations, the Lifesaving Service was founded in 1871 for the purpose of protecting the lives of those in peril on the sea or along its beaches. The stations polka-dotting the American shoreline were each composed of eight surf men under the supervision of a keeper who was the station's officer-in-charge. The West Coast stations were initially under jurisdiction of the 13th Lifesaving District superintendent located at San Francisco.

Stations were equipped with a surf boat and a lifeboat, sometimes only the former, a Lyle (line throwing) gun, a breeches buoy, a beach cart, faking box (in which the line for the Lyle gun was stored), life preservers, medical kits, Coston flares, axes, shovels, lanterns, picks, shovels and a "slop chest" full of clothes for survivors. Surf men worked a six day week on a rotation basis, six having to be present at all times, as that was the number, plus the steersman (usually the keeper) it took to man the pulling craft. The stations that had volunteer crews usually employed only the keeper, and it was his responsibility to round up the volunteers whenever a ship was in distress.

At some stations, personnel patrolled the beaches carrying a lantern and Coston flares at night, the latter used for signaling the station should a ship in trouble be sighted.

Not until 1908 were gasoline-powered rescue craft introduced to West Coast stations.

Surf men were often called on to launch their boats into crashing breakers swollen by driving winds even in the dead of night. Very often it took suicidal efforts to save terror-stricken mariners or passengers trapped on ships being torn to pieces on jagged outcrops. With none of the sophisticated lifesaving equipment of the present day, it was strictly a case of men against the sea.

Famous photograph of the Columbia River bar probably at its wildest. The ship behind huge swell, the *Colonel de Villebois Marieul*, is under tow of the tug boat *Tatoosh*. This was in 1912.

Bleached ribs of many ships lie half buried in the Oregon beach sands while at the bases of the rocky monoliths, torn and mangled hulks rest in the silent depths. Occasionally, from the beaches, the remains of forgotten wrecks will reappear like ghosts and, in a short time vanish again under the shifting sands.

True grit was the stuff of which many of the old-time surf men were made. One of the bravest working the Oregon coast was Captain John Bergman. He was a man of amazing endurance, courage and leadership. Born in Germany in 1847, he had been a seafarer from the age of 15.

A wreck during the bleak January of 1883 is an example of his ability. Here is the drama that was to include Captain Bergman as the man of the hour.

Steaming southward on the second leg of her maiden voyage, the half-million dollar steam collier *Tacoma,* out of Puget Sound, rode low in the water with more than 3,500 tons of Carbonado coal destined for San Francisco. The officers were:

> George D. Kortz, Captain – Master
> L. L. Simmons, First officer
> C. Rodman, Second officer
> R. H. Willoughby, Third officer
> H. Wilson, Chief Engineer

There was apprehension aboard over the sour complexion of the weather. All Oregon coast landmarks had been obliterated.

Pitching and rolling under her heavy burden, the *Tacoma* strained in her every joint. Captain Kortz had confidence in his new vessel that was fresh out of the builder's yard in Philadelphia. Due to her excellent speed and maneuverability, the ship-master believed she could literally walk on water. But this was a most unusual night with the dull throb of the engines totally drowned out by the howling winds and crashing seas as the vessel passed through the darkness like a mysterious shadow.

Toward 9 p.m., in the dim light of the wheel house, the officers discussed the ship's position with the quartermaster. All agreed with the skipper that they were a comfortable distance offshore and should be in no danger, therefore full speed was maintained. Unfortunately, their combined intelligence was in-adequate. Within a few minutes there was a grinding crash. The steamer vibrated from stem to stern suddenly reeling like one who is inebriated. The sickening grating of steel against rock left little question about the seriousness of the encounter.

The vessel had gone from full-ahead to a dead stop in what seemed like a split-second. Anything not bolted down went askew. Most of the crew were knocked flat on the deck or hurled from their bunks. As if a beehive had been disturbed, every man was suddenly scurrying about, the skipper shouting into the speaking tube for the engineer to give the engine full thrust astern.

No one aboard the *Tacoma* was at first sure what the ship had struck nor would they know until dawn. In truth, the steamer had collided with a reef close to shore just four miles north of the Umpqua River.

Despite the full power of the engine, the steamer remained as if in a vice. The crew, some in near panic and many half clothed, went about unorganized. The whistle started to blast its mournful sound over the storm-shrouded ocean.

Walls of salt-water boarded the vessel running like mighty rivers down the slanting decks and out through the scuppers. Flames in kerosene lamps flickered and died. Breaks in the steel plates grew larger as the hull strained. Pipes broke and steam hissed as the vessel gasped for life.

Kortz tried to keep some kind of order until the damage could be surveyed by daylight, but as water crept up around the boilers, the fires went out emitting massive billows of steam climbing from below. Night seemed an eternity. Nobody ate or slept.

With dawn, the situation was observed to be worse than the captain had imagined. The hull had been battered below the waterline and coal was spewing out of the flooded holds. The engine room was inundated and the main deck looked as if had been hit by a hurricane. All but one of the lifeboats had been either stove or carried overboard. With no aid in sight, if there was to be any action it would have to start with those aboard and it had to be immediate.

Under extreme difficulty, Captain Kortz and six of his men managed to get the one usable boat lowered over the lee side. Contrary to the usual custom of the sea, the shipmaster decided to try for shore to get assistance for his vessel rather than to remain till the bitter end. Narrowly missing being smashed like an eggshell, the boat freed itself of the wreck, then with backs and arms straining to the uttermost, the oarsmen challenged the mountainous breakers. With Kortz at the steering sweep, the craft made a phenomenal run in closing the 400 yards between the wreck and the beach. Almost broaching, the lifeboat was carried high up on the sands, the occupants stumbling out drenched to the skin. Almost immediately, a giant curling sea snatched the craft away and smashed it to kindling on the nearby rocks. The last link with those on the *Tacoma* had been broken.

After a stumbling hike through the driving rain and buffeting by the wind, the shipmaster and his men finally reached the little lumber town of Gardiner, a few miles up the Umpqua River. Whenever a ship was in trouble, everybody in town dropped whatever they were doing and headed for the scene.

In 1883, the government had not yet established an official life saving station on the Umpqua so everything was voluntary. With food, spirits, blankets and medicines, the citizens of the town hurried to the beach opposite the wreck. Driftwood fires were kindled, a dory was hauled to the beach by a mule team in the hope it could be launched into the breakers; all of this in the face of the chilling wind and rain that continued unabated.

With the start of another day, those keeping the vigil could see that the steamer had broken in half. The survivors had taken refuge in the dining saloon but when the bulkheads parted they were forced out on the open deck to hang doggedly on to anything solid enough to resist the relentless seas that pummeled the ship. The thermometer kept going down, and the leaden canopy above was dropping a freezing sleet that, in the wind, drove almost horizontally. Ice formed on the twisted rigging and visibility was barely a quarter mile. The surf was in such condition that it would have taken a miracle to reach the wreck. It was sheer agony for those who waited.

The tug, *Sol Thomas*, Captain Lawson, put to sea to try to get a line to the wreck. Though successful in surmounting the wrath of the river entrance, Lawson was unable to get close enough to the wreck to fire a line. Plunging and rolling like a cork, the *Sol Thomas* could do nothing but stand helplessly by.

In the interim, some of the local citizens walked southward along the beach to Coos Bay where there was a lifesaving station in the lee of an islet on which stood Cape Arago lighthouse. The post of keeper, (a government employee) was held by Captain James Desmond. A recently established facility, funds had not allowed for a paid staff of lifesaving personnel; therefore volunteers were used in emergencies. The Umpqua party requested the immediate services of the craft to rescue the men on the *Tacoma*. At the same time, the tug *Escort No. 2,* Captain Magee, on Coos Bay, was enlisted to meet and tow the surf boat to the wreck scene. The two vessels were to rendezvous off Cape Arago.

Volunteers responding to the call to man surf boat were C. E. Getty, Tom Hall, Joe Collumber, George Wilson, Andrew Jackson, George Morris, L. Geiger and C. B. Watson, in addition to Captain Desmond.

Two days had now passed since the wreck. The seas had battered the *Tacoma* into near submission as now only the masts and stack still stood defiantly in the blasting wind.

Another volunteer, Chandler B. Watson, later wrote:

The new surf boat had never before been taken out and the hatches and tackle having been kept painted, were stiff and hard to handle. The boat was a splendid specimen of that class of craft, and with its cargo of necessary equipment, was heavy. By midnight the boat was on the beach with life-line, cannon to shoot the line, life preservers etc. all stored and ready to push off so soon as the tide should serve. It was yet four hours before the tug was expected which would be about daylight. If one can imagine it, the storm was gradually increasing

Desmond, the keeper of the station and ex-officio captain of the crew, appeared to be nervous and frankly admitted that our undertaking was a perilous one. We examined the lashings, put on our life suits, assumed the stations assigned to us and 'stood by' ready to receive orders. We were instructed to stand at our places with our oars in the sands to steady the boat and when the word should be given, to drop to our seats and shove off. The boat's nose was kept on the sands and its stem out toward the channel.

The water was breaking in 30 fathoms and waves were rolling tumultuously – great combers glowing with phosphorescent light seemed to be miles in length. As a huge breaker rose before the men, the order to back on the oars was obeyed.

The tug had not yet come in sight and the captain made an excuse to go back to the station. Everything was put in trim and awaited the captain knowing that the tug would soon whistle on arrival to pickup the tow. After half an hour and no captain, I took another man and went to the station to ascertain the cause of the delay. We found him snugly ensconced behind the stove and in answer to us, he declared that all the money in Christendom would not induce him to go out into that surf again. Here was a man who had been entrusted with the responsibilities of life-saving keeper, on the first occasion of his services being called for, and in the most critical moment, showing the white feather when his crew of volunteers were clamoring to do this act of generosity and mercy. We begged, argued, entreated and finally threatened, but all to no purpose.

Going out again, we saw the tug about a riffle away and from the steam from her whistle we knew she was blowing for us. We secured another [smaller boat] from the lighthouse keeper and sent two men off to the tug to announce the situation and to ask the captain to send the tug's boat in with the crew that had volunteered and we would meet them with the lifeboat. The proposition was refused. The trip out in the small, leaky boat, in such a surf was a very hard, dangerous mission, but those two men were brave men, and it was our purpose to take the lifeboat out to them [on the *Tacoma*] ourselves, when with astonishment we saw the tug deliberately turn and disappear over the bar.

The mission was accordingly scrubbed.

It looked like a shocking piece of cowardice all round. We knew, however, that the captain of the tug was no coward but up to this day [written in 1929] there had been no satisfactory explanation offered. *

Meanwhile back at the wreck scene, the survival of those on the *Tacoma* rested with the people of Gardiner. Where an outright show of cowardice had been displayed by the boat captain at Cape Arago, a hero was being born with the name of John Bergman. Despite overwhelming odds, he directed rescue operations from the beach and was willing to go one step further than any of the volunteers who aided him. Throughout the second and third days, a small dory-like craft was repeatedly launched into the savage surf, but each time it capsized spilling its occupants into the chilling surf. Time after time, Bergman ordered the craft righted, bailed out and re-launched. Always encouraging his cohorts, he would point to the wreck, just 400 tormenting yards away. Both frustrated and exhausted, Bergman seemed possessed of superhuman strength. With little food and hours without sleep, his driving determination paid off on the third day when the rescue craft negotiated the surf by virtually standing on

---

* Watson was of the opinion that James Desmond should have gone to prison for his refusal to man the surf boat but as it turned out, after several days' investigation, the boat keeper was merely relieved of his position and replaced by a seasoned and able keeper named William Abbott.

end. Pulling on the oars, the men gave it their all braving the tempest, at last reaching the sorry pile of wreckage. Pitiful survivors watched grimly praying to be rescued. Suffering terribly from cold and hunger, they stood like frozen statues. In a miraculous piece of seamanship the dory, bucking like a Brahma bull, managed to work in on the lee side of the reef. So anxious were those waiting that they made a stampede for the craft as it came alongside. Had not first assistant engineer J. K. Grant kept order with his pistol, the craft could have swamped. It was a tense moment. Only a limited number of survivors could be accommodated. Tears filled the eyes of those left behind. Every man not at an oar had to bail constantly.

With Bergman steering, the rescue craft came in through the breakers to the beach where volunteers, wading out to their armpits to assist, helped them ashore. Women on the beach received them, ten in all.

No sooner was the first mission accomplished than Bergman and his recruits were on their way out through the surf for more survivors. The craft was successful in picking up another group, but on the way in, tragedy intervened. Before the eyes of those on the beach, a giant wall of water snatched the rescue boat, flipped it into the air, then dropped it rudely into the trough, its people flung out to fight for survival in the troubled sea. Those from the ship, terribly weakened by exposure and hunger, could struggle no longer. Again volunteers waded into the surf to lend a hand.

Among those pulled in was first assistant engineer Grant. He was placed gently on the sands above the driftwood line and covered with blankets. Pale and drawn, eyes like hollow sockets, his heart finally gave out.

Still on the battered wreck, nine waited their turn to be rescued. Continuing to standby offshore was the *Sol Thomas* seeking a chance to get a line to the wreck, but that opportunity never came.

Thursday morning arrived. The storm had abated for a few hours but was only gathering new breath to fill its powerful lungs. The seas continued massive and treacherous, a threat to any who would challenge. A second tug arrived on the scene, the *Fearless,* skippered by Captain James Hill, which had steamed north from

Coos Bay.

For those who clung to their miserable perches aboard the *Tacoma,* three days and four nights had passed without food or warm clothing, in totally adverse weather. The nightmarish experience must have been such that even death would seem welcome. And death it was, for no other rescue craft was to reach the side of the wreck until the last life had flickered and died.

On the other hand, 18 survivors owed their lives to the courage and stamina of John Bergman and his volunteers. Had it not been for the cowardice of James Desmond, the lives of the unfortunates might have been spared. Every calamity produces its heroes and cowards and in this incident there were extremes of both.

*   *   *

A lighthouse had been placed at the entrance to the Umpqua River by Uncle Sam as early as 1857, first on the Oregon Coast but unfortunately, the tower was built on sand and with the river freshets and the scouring effects of the tides, the foundation was undermined and the structure, in 1861, tumbled to the ground.

From 1861 till 1894, the government frowned on a replacement despite constant agitation by maritime interests along the Oregon coast. Weak political representation was obvious. All through that "dark" period, many navigation charts continued to show a lighthouse at the location lacking any notation of its destruction. Whether or not the presence of a lighthouse could have prevented the loss of the *Tacoma* remains speculative.

*   *   *

Nine years after the loss of the *Tacoma,* Captain John Bergman, then in charge of the U. S. Lifesaving Service's new Umpqua Station at Gardiner, was recognized for his brave work. Presented the coveted gold lifesaving medal, he became a legend in his own time. The members of his volunteer boat crew in the *Tacoma* rescue mission were also cited for their bravery.

If nothing else good came out of the tragedy, the *Tacoma* wreck did much toward allotting government funds for the lifesaving station on the Umpqua River.

Salvage tug *Salvage Chief* after modernization. This vessel now has no steering wheel – is steered with levers. She was launched as a landing craft in World War II and has been on hundreds of salvage jobs.

Captain Bergman retired in Florence, Oregon after a long and illustrious career. He died at the ripe old age of 92 having outlived his Swiss wife, who had borne him seven children and having married twice after that. At his funeral services the words that accompanied the awarding of his gold medal were read again, Coast Guard pallbearers proudly carrying his body to its final resting place. ☐

Chapter 8
Bars, Jetties and the
U. S. Army Engineers

$\mathbf{A}$ look at the map of the United States will reveal that Oregon has the straightest coastline of any major maritime state in the union. Most access to harbors is through bar openings and good commercial portals are few. Bar entrances require constant repair. Without jetties and properly maintained bar depths, nature's forces would win the battle and marine graveyards would be far better stocked than at present.

Synonymous with improved navigation on the Oregon coast is the Portland District of the U. S. Army Corps of Engineers. A century ago, the work of the District consisted of small, simple, almost quaint efforts to improve navigation, according to Colonel Robert L. Bangert. He cited the pulling of snags from river waterways, cutting bars 17 feet deep with primitive bucket dredges or dynamiting rocks out of the Columbia River as representative of work done in those early years. By comparison with today, the agency maintains all of the main ocean bar entrances and jetties with federal funds and has tackled the building of massive complex dams on the Columbia, the Willamette and on the Snake Rivers, plus a host of navigational projects that run annually into the multi-millions of dollars. That branch of the service has been beneficial to the state of Oregon.

The Corps traces its origin to the earliest days of the republic, when on June 16, 1775, the day before the Battle of Bunker Hill, George Washington created the first engineering unit in the Army. Its services did not become active on the Oregon coast until 1866. In that year, Congress initiated a series of River and Harbor Acts

Imperial Japanese submarine of the aircraft-carrying type, that shelled Fort Stevens on June 21, 1941. The airplane was launched less than 90 days later, September 29, when the pilot, using Cape Blanco light house as his fix, bombed the Siskiyou National Forest and started a forest fire.*

which made the Corps responsible for the development and maintenance of all officially designated federal waterways. These include Oregon's ten major coastal rivers. Early works included fortifications as well as public works and the construction of lighthouses. Fort Stevens was constructed just south of the Columbia River. It was ineffectually shelled by a Japanese submarine during World War II making it the only U. S. continental fort to be fired on since the War of 1812.*

To date, the Army Engineers have constructed 22 jetties on the ten major Oregon rivers, plus accompanying navigation channels on eight of them. If placed end-to-end, the total length of these jetties is 28 miles. Individual lengths range from 6.6 miles on the south jetty of the Columbia River entrance to .24 miles on the north Chetco project in Southern Oregon. These jetties contain nearly 27 million tons of rock and concrete fill which if stacked on a football field would tower skyward more than a mile and a half.

Taxpayers have doled out more than $100 million dollars for these Oregon projects – moneys well spent as the end product is invaluable to the maritime industry and to the public. Commerce, the trade of the world, reaches into every household of Oregon and to every citizen.

---

* The details are in *Silent Siege III: Japanese Attacks On North America in WWII; Ships Sunk, Air raids, Bombs Dropped, Civilians Killed.* See bibliography.

Though Oregon coast projects are only a segment of the Army Engineers' Portland District program, it is the segment that is dealt with here. The growing importance of the Columbia and Willamette rivers as navigational waterways led to the establishment of the Portland District in 1871. Without improvements on these rivers, the development of commerce in the region would halt. Major Henry M. Robert, the first Portland District Engineer, is however most remembered for his authorship and publication of *Robert's Rules of Order.** He was directed to establish an office in Portland and resume work under the authorization, *Improvement of Rivers in Oregon.*

Going back even further in history, the first engineers sent by the military to Oregon country were at the beginning of the 19th century. It was the Louisiana Purchase that linked the history of Oregon with the activities of the Corps of Engineers.

After negotiations with France for the purchase had been completed, President Thomas Jefferson appointed two Army Captains, Meriwether Lewis and William Clark, to lead an expedition across the uncharted territory now owned by the United States. The purpose was to see exactly what they had bought. Until that time, little was known of the Pacific Northwest since Captain Robert Gray's discovery of the river in 1792. Tales from trappers who had dared venture west and legends of the Indians formed the total sum of intelligence on the area .

The object of the Lewis and Clark Expedition was to find, "the most direct and practicable water communication across this continent." The appointment was to go west to the end of the territory, but once there, the team of officers and helpers decided to proceed to the Pacific Ocean. Accordingly, this expedition has been called the longest overland hiking adventure at government expense in the history of the United States. It was a highly successful enterprise.

Beginning in the spring of 1804, the expedition progressed up the Missouri River to its headwaters, portaged to waters of the

---

* As a young Lieutenant, Robert was one of the Corps of Engineers Officers assigned to building the American fort on San Juan Island where the British had brought up its Navy and the U. S. Army its troops because a Yankee farmer had killed a British pig. The day-to-day excitement is in *The Pig War; The Journal of William A. Peck*. See bibliography.

Columbia, and canoed to its mouth. The winter of 1805-06 was spent at the mouth of the Columbia, where the party erected Fort Clatsop. The first direct contact these explorers had with the Oregon Coast was their camp on the beach at what is now the City of Seaside. This camp was established for the purpose of collecting and boiling sea water to obtain salt.

The two Army captains put their backgrounds in engineering and science to work not only in forging their way across the wild country but in recording the nature of the land they encountered.

Until 1824, the Corps had worked mainly on military projects. Some public works were done, mainly navigation projects, but the President was as likely to assign the work to private concerns as to the Corps of Engineers.

With the close of the Civil War in 1865, an age of tremendous growth was experienced. On the establishment in 1866 of the authority, "Rivers and Harbors of the Pacific Coast," Army Engineer activities in the far west were on an equal footing with the rest of the nation for the first time. San Francisco was the location of the office, and its authority included all the Pacific Northwest, Brevet Lieutenant Colonel R. S. Williamson becoming the first District Engineer.

Where early Oregon coast work is concerned, the name that stands out above all others is Major G. L. Gillespie. For three years, from October 1878 until July 1881, when he was District Engineer in Portland, there was considerable activity and progress. In 1901 he became Chief of Engineers. He played a large part in the supervision of the Cascades Canal on the Columbia River and the construction of Tillamook Rock Light Station,* one of the nation's greatest engineering feats, plus improvements at Coos Bay, Coquille River and Yaquina Bay.

The public seldom thinks about why jetties, that control the river entrances to Oregon ports, are necessary and what it took to place them where they are. Of the ten projects of great commercial value, some were completed before the turn of the

---

* The startling story of the building and operation of Tillamook Rock Lighthouse is in *Terrible Tilly; Tillamook Rock Lighthouse; a Biography of a Lighthouse – An Oregon Documentary*. See bibliography.

century. Though all have undergone rebuilding from time to time, some of the basic original layouts remain. In addition, the agency has completed many small-boat basins on the Oregon coast. Outstanding is the construction of a breakwater to establish a basin at Port Orford. The Corps is also responsible for the harbor entrance and facilities at Depoe Bay, probably the smallest "doghole" commercial port in the continental United States.

One of the most unique projects of the Corps was the construction of a dike at Bayocean just south of Tillamook Bay entrance. This was after coastal erosion tore down the sand spit and destroyed the town.*

rial view of Depoe Bay on north Oregon Coast. This port, the
allest in the world, hosts a fleet of private boats, fishing
arter fleets and the Coast Guard.

---

*Refer to *Bayocean, The Oregon Town That Fell Into the Sea.* See bibliography.

**Major Oregon Coast jetty projects
and their completion dates:**

Columbia River:
South jetty, completed in 1895
North jetty completed in 1917
Spur jetty "A" completed in 1939

Nehalem Bay jetty: completed in 1918 (reconstructed 1980's)

Tillamook Bay:
Channel to Miami River completed in 1927
North jetty first phase 1917; completed in 1927
South jetty authorized 1965 - completed 1974
Bayocean dike completed in 1956
Small-boat basin, Garibaldi, completed in 1958

Yaquina Bay and Harbor:
South jetty completed in 1888
North jetty completed in 1896

Siuslaw River
North and South jetties completed in 1917
Channel completed in 1930

Umpqua River:
North jetty completed in 1919
South jetty completed in 1933
Training jetty completed in 1950

Coos Bay:
North and South jetties completed in 1928-29
Channel dredged to 24 feet in 1937

Coquille River:
North and South jetties completed in 1908
Entrance channel completed in 1933

Rogue River:
North and South jetties completed in 1960

Chetco River:
North and South jetties completed in 1957.

Diplomacy, always a factor in Corps of Engineers planning, has become quite profound with the emphasis on environmental issues.

Every project must be looked at from two sides:

1. The commercial value of the ports at the river entrances
2. The need for preservation of estuaries of the coastal rivers.

Sometimes the Corps has to grit its teeth because the coastal region embraces these two factors.

An estuary includes all the area where ocean salt water mingles with fresh water. Here the tides pump in rich supplies of nutrients and oxygen from the ocean while the fresh water flow removes waste materials. In many places, solar radiation penetrates shallow tidal waters to allow abundant vegetation to grow. The result is a unique feeding and spawning ground for many forms of marine life that are important links in the food chain.

Some 217 square miles of the Oregon coast are occupied as estuaries. A proper balance is called for where nature and man-made use of these unique ecosystems must be carefully managed.

The Corps engages in a dredging program to keep Oregon's coastal harbors open to commercial and recreational navigation. The proposed dredging sites are carefully reviewed in advance. Federal and state environmental and fishery agencies as well as public input are considered before decisions are announced.

Wherever possible, the dredging material or spoils are utilized to provide or enhance wildlife and marine life habitat. Special procedures are followed to minimize the impact of dredging on the natural environment. In addition, the Engineers are always involved in research, locally and nationally, and administer a permit program to protect coastal and river environments.

The authority given to that body originated with the River and Harbor Act of 1899 which allows no dredging or construction in navigable waters without, at that time, permission of the Secretary of the Army. That act, handled with tact and authority, is still valid after nearly a century. The original intent was aimed at navigation right-of-way but now includes environmental considerations. Today, any public or private concern wishing to build or dredge in coastal or river waters must apply for a permit.

In the early to middle 1800's, navigation from the ocean into the Oregon coastal rivers was extremely dangerous if not impossible. Because of this, the Oregon coast claimed hundreds of ships. Every river deposited large quantities of sand and sediment at their respective mouths and would build up hazardous spits or bars that literally crawled across the entrances. This natural phenomenon made navigation charts that were accurate one year erroneous for the next.

Channels constantly changed causing shipwreck that took a huge toll in lives and property. These conditions demanded that skippers of vessels have nerves of steel and a sixth sense in order to make successful bar crossings especially with ships of sail where the winds were a basic factor. The portals which catered to the greatest volume in commerce claimed the most ships back when the bars were in their raw condition – no jetties – the best example being the entrance to the Columbia River.

Many doughty mariners in the early years would argue that the Coquille River bar was the most hazardous, especially when a sailing vessel lost the wind while in transit. The difficulty at the Coquille was shifting sand and rock obstruction. The survey completed in the summer of 1878 was done by Assistant Engineer Channing M. Bolton. He learned from the pilot at the Coquille, Captain Reicker, that:

> The sands shift so rapidly that I cannot rely on information from one day to the next, but have to make a thorough examination of the channel before each trip.

A request was made for $164,000 to build two training walls, two to three thousand feet long, to run parallel to each other along the deepest section of the existing channel extending into deep water. The plan was to increase velocity of the outflowing river due to the contraction of the channel to keep it scoured to a depth of 12 feet.

Work continued under Major Gillespie in 1880 after the plan by Major Wilson was revised. Within two years, the jetty had reached a length of 850 feet and by 1886 was 2,000 feet long. (This was in the days before bulldozers and trucks.) Two years later, the $215,000 jetty was completed. By 1908, a second jetty was finished.

At Coos Bay a survey made under Major Wilson in 1878, showed that obstructions to navigation were caused by shifting sands and by unpredictable tides. A detailed chart was made of the entrance, then plans called for construction of two jetties to cost $972,000. The Board of Engineers accepted the findings but ruled that only one wall would be built at a cost not to exceed $600,000. Work got underway during Major Gillespie's tenure in

1879, but quickly ran into trouble. It was found that the floor of the bar was too rocky to permit pile driving. To overcome this obstacle, timber cribs were built to hold the heavy rock. After two years, only 700 feet of the cribbing had been put in place. Gillespie called for more funds in 1881. He stated:

...if better water in the lower harbor and more direct channel over the bar can be maintained, all the lumber interests bordering the bay will be increased in value, the mills will be kept running throughout the year..., the improvement will be of benefit to all Southern Oregon, for at the present time this is the only port south of the Columbia River from which there is a regular line south and from which lumber is shipped in noteworthy quantities. It is possible to build up here a very important trade not only with San Francisco, but with the islands of the Pacific which give a demand for lumber and the various kinds of excellent timber.

Work dragged on until completed in 1889 due to slow receipt of funds and damage to the jetty and tramway caused by excessive seas. But Coos Bay emerged as the most important port on the Oregon Coast. This was a giant of a job with the total project not completed until 1929. The bar was deepened to 24 feet in 1937.

A third project under Gillespie's reign was at Yaquina Bay. Surveys made in 1879, and again in the spring of 1880, called for a 2,500 foot jetty drawn up by Assistant Engineer J. S. Polhemus. The bay entrance had been limited to only seven feet by a sand spit and outer shoals. Gillespie said of the bay:

If a depth of 17 feet on the bar at high tide can be maintained by improvement, the harbor will become a shipping port of great importance, not only for the products raised in the immediate vicinity, but for a great part of the Upper Willamette Valley, with which it is said that there will soon be a railroad connection.

The plan was approved in July 1880 and in the same year an initial appropriation of $40,000 was forthcoming. But progress seemed unreasonably slow. According to Major Gillespie:

The village of Newport, in the harbor, is very small and at the time the assistant engineer took charge of the improvement, the single sawmill which the bay possessed was out of order and had no logs on hand suitable for the construction. In consequence, considerable time was spent collecting logs before any lumber for the scows or timber for the cribs could be obtained, and all the various materials and implements of construction – iron, anchors, picks, chains, crowbars, oakum etc. – had to be purchased either at Portland or

Twin jetties at mouth of Yaquina Bay. For other views of the historic bridge seen in the background, see pages 23 and 34.

San Francisco and sent to the harbor by special boats. These considerations not only made the initial preparations very expensive but delayed – much beyond my patience – the time of the beginning of the jetty.

The entrance of the Yaquina harbor was considered so dangerous that no tugboat captain was willing to hire out and assist the work, so a tug boat had to be purchased in San Francisco.

The exceedingly strong and variable currents at Yaquina Bay presented the party with the greatest imaginable difficulties. Work in boats became impractical and the assistant engineer (Polhemus) elected to build the jetty from the shore outward. He stated :

Jetties at mouth of the Rogue River. Cities of Wedderburn on left, Gold Beach on right. There has been extensive real estate development since 1969 when this view was made. For another picture of the historic bridge in background, see page 165.

...the stone for the purpose had to be delivered by a tramway 2,500 feet long starting from a wharf erected in a sheltered spot on the inside of the harbor. This plan necessitates the handling of the stone four times but I see no other way of accomplishing the desired end.

This method was used for the next seven years by Polhemus until the initial south jetty was completed in 1888. Actually, the north jetty was not completed until 1896. As difficult as that was, it became the first double jetty on the Oregon coast. *

Gillespie was still District Engineer when the initial work on the Columbia River was begun. The River and Harbor Act of 1878 had authorized an examination at the mouth of the Columbia to determine the nature and cost of permanent developments. Major Gillespie reported the following year:

---

* At Yaquina Bay, the rock ordered was basalt but as it was not sufficiently sturdy, that part of the work had to be repeated with granite. For the story of this and of the lighthouses there, refer to *Yaquina Lighthouses on the Oregon Coast*. See bibliography.

101

It is impossible to give an estimate of the extent to which commerce will be benefited by this improvement. Should an improvement be adopted for the harbor which will give an increased depth of water over the bar and enable vessels drawing 22 to 23 feet of water to cross without danger at all stages of the tide, the commerce of the whole Northwest will be increased beyond the capabilities of anyone to estimate at the present time.

Even in the 1876-1878 period, total value of exports crossing over the Columbia River bar amounted to nearly $20 million. Gillespie stated:

The citizens of Astoria are anxious that some extensive improvement should be undertaken in hand to increase the depth of water over the bar.

With the mouth of the river in its natural state, the tides and currents from the ocean plus the current of the Columbia itself, could almost overnight alter the entrance to the river. Charts dating back several decades showed that two channels existed at the mouth of the river. The difficulty lay in the fact that of these channels, neither was of sufficient depth nor dependable enough to guarantee safe bar transit. This was especially true during bad weather.

Only the most foolhardy of skippers dared cross without the aid of a pilot or a tugboat. In the 1878-1881 period, several vessels became victims of the bar. Channel depth changed abruptly and the 17 to 21-foot depth was never certain over a period of time.

In 1880, Gillespie submitted a plan for an 8,000-foot jetty at the river's south entrance. This, compared with the other Oregon jetties, was almost three times as long, and the cost was estimated at the sum of $4,750,000. In those days (long before income taxes), this was mighty big money. The Congress, when such funds were requested, shook in its collective boots. The project was designed to obtain a secure, deep channel by concentrating the current of the river and the tidal action of the sea. The request was denied by the board of review.

Oregon business interests were furious. Businessmen and politicians clamped on the pressure until the plan was reviewed by the board at the order of Congress. The west was being opened, and a blueprint even more grandiose than Gillespie's was adopted. Citizens sent evidence of the large number of shipwrecks, while

Siuslaw River entrance in 1969 view. The jetties have since been repaired and extended.

maritime interests argued the commercial value of river commerce. As a result, the mammoth south jetty was completed in 1895 and the north jetty in 1917. Until the 1930's this was the largest project undertaken by the Portland District.

The massive Columbia River jetties have been rebuilt many times and the present 48-foot bar depth on the Columbia is far beyond the dreams of the early Army Engineers.

Back in 1884-1885, when the south jetty work was in its infancy, the equivalent of a small town had to be set up to accomodate the project. Men had to be hired, materials ordered, delivered then appropriately stored on site. Offices, shops and a dock were constructed then an approach trestle from the beach completed. A quarry site for the rock was chosen then housing and mess facilities installed. Then the final survey was made but the 1886 appropriation was a mere $170,000. Two years were to pass until Congress coughed up another $500,000. Still more money – much more – was needed therefore it took ten years and $4 million to complete the jetty. When finished in 1895, it

SS Oliver Olson, **making for the Coquille River on November 2, 1953, ploughed into the end of the south jetty. After partial salvage, the hull was filled with rock and the ship became part of the jetty.**

measured 30 feet at its crest and from 80 to 90 feet along the base. The bar depth was about 31 feet.

Though the bar depth was gradually increased to 36-37 feet at the entrance, continued shoaling demanded a second jetty. The decision was made to proceed with construction of the north jetty to bring the project depth to a reliable 40 feet. Cost of the 2½ mile jetty was to be about $6 million. Actual construction was started in 1914, with Kern & Kern as general contractors, under the direction of the Army Corps of Engineers.

Adventurous visitors sometimes climb along the rough rocks of the south jetty to exposed remains of the *Oliver Olson*. Such a hike is not without risk. In this case, a breaker crashed against the jetty showering Rick Webber, former Coast Guardsman, as well as the cameraman.

The job was finished in 1917 and the survey proved right the bar depth gradually exceeding the planned 40 feet. When completed, the Columbia River jetties were the largest in the world and for the first time, there was an almost sure guarantee of safe transit provided all of the prevailing rules were followed.

After completion of the north jetty, District Engineer Lt. Colonel C. H. McKinstry reported:

> The improvement has made it possible for the largest vessels operating on the Pacific Coast to enter and leave at all normal stages of tide in any weather except during the most severe storms. Bar-bound vessels, once so common are now, on account of improved conditions, rarely to be seen.

Portland marine interests with the improvement of the bar strongly recommended the deepening of the Columbia and Willamette Rivers to Portland (100 miles). This project, through the years, has been a major endeavor. Without a deep river channel, all vessels would have to unload at least part of their cargoes at Astoria.

All of the bar projects on the Oregon coast presented difficulties for the builders. Often winter storms did irreparable damage. In addition, when large funds were requested for bar projects in the early years, the Engineers found that many of the solons in Washington D. C. were totally ignorant of the maritime needs of the west coast. Whenever the word "Oregon" was mentioned, many thought only of Indians and were reluctant to pass sufficient funds to complete projects.

In 1880 when Major Bolton recommended that $200,000 would have to be spent for the jetties at the entrance to the Coquille River, the political giants raised their eyebrows.

"Where's the Coquille?" asked one.

"Never heard of the place," exclaimed another.

The major explained that without the aid of the jetties the Coquille, portal to vast stands of timber, was extremely dangerous. Through the work of some tireless individuals, $20,000 was squeezed from Uncle Sam to begin the project.

*   *   *

The first commercial schooner crossed the Coos Bay bar in 1852 with great difficulty. The initial vessel to bring cargo across

(Top) Loading rock for the Columbia River north jetty about 1916.
(Lower) Rocks being dumped from rail cars for building the jetty.

the bar was, the *Cynosure,* skippered by Captain Whippy, in 1853. He send out a small boat to seek a proper channel but the rough seas capsized the craft and all of its occupants were drowned. The *Cynosure* finally got across the bar with its supplies for the newly opened Randolph mines.

Casualties were numerous at the entrance to Coos Bay, second only to those of the Columbia River bar. Between the 1850's and 1880's many familiar commercial carriers came to grief. These included:

Cohansa	1850's	Noyo	1868
Chancey	1854	D. M. Hall	1868
Quadratus	1856	Ida M. Rogers	1869
Jackson	1857	Charles Devens	1870
New World	1857	Commodore	1870
Cyclops	1862	Fearless	1873
Energy	1862	Gussie Telfair	1880

A U. S. Revenue Cutter, the brig *Captain Lincoln*, was driven aground, a few miles north of Coos Bay. The vessel sprang a leak in heavy seas before coming to her final resting place. The survivors, a detachment of soldiers, set up a camp where they could carefully watch the actions of the Indians. They named the place Camp Castaway.

The ill-fated vessel had sailed from San Francisco Dec. 28, 1851 with C Troop of the First Dragoons under command of Lt. H. W. Stanton. The destination was Port Orford. Instead, the ship was driven north of her destination by a persistent storm, grinding to an unscheduled stop on Jan. 3, 1852.

Camp Castaway existed for the remainder of the winter before the troops abandoned the site and marched southward along the beaches. The Indians, though curious, remained passive during the entire operation.

These and numerous other marine disasters led to early efforts for bar and navigation improvements along the Oregon coast because the fickle temperaments of the bar entrances were a serious blockade to the growth of waterborne commerce. In many cases, shipmasters refused to risk crossings except under the most favorable conditions. The answer, in most cases, was to construct jetties. When jetties are built, entrance into a river by ships is considerably eased. This concentrated water flow scours out shallow sand deposits and stabilizes the river channel. Combined with periodic dredging, jetties provide a safe route from ocean to river.

Construction techniques have evolved over the years as machines that would handle the work became available. The brief description of building a jetty begins, generally, with a bed of rocks placed on the ocean floor. Larger boulders are placed atop

Like old shoes, jetties also wear out as shown at entrance of Nehalem Bay. The old original work, completed in 1918, has now been rebuilt.

this bed to form the main body of the jetty. Boulders get progressively larger toward the jetty's seaward end where wave action is the most powerful. Here rocks, up to and over 30 tons each, are used to resist the perpetual onslaught of the sea.

Prior to the 1950's, jetty rocks were hauled to placement sites by rail dump cars. Some of the older jetties still have the remains of the wooden trestles which supported the little steam locomotives that rolled on rails pulling rock-laden dump cars.

Today rock is hauled by off-road size dump trucks and placed by large self-propelled cranes.

As we have seen, although jetties stabilize and deepen river channels, they do not entirely solve the matter. Each river continues to pour tons of sediment downstream. In order to keep the bar channels and harbors clear, dredging is essential. A navigation channel provides a deep water path through the river bar and upstream to the port area.

Each year from May through October, government dredges move millions of yards of sediment from coastal river channels.

U. S. Army Corps of Engineers dredge *Biddle* for years kept harbor entrances cleared for shipping.

This dredging is accomplished by vessels that vacuum sediment off the bottom. Hopper dredges are built with compartments which store the dredged material then later dump it at sea or in some other predetermined place. Pipeline dredges, often operated by private contractors, transport the dredged material through large pipes to deposit sites on shore

In one unique situation, sand was dredged from the bottom of Tillamook Bay not to deepen the bay but to obtain material to rebuild the spit after erosion had ripped it out.

On that occurrence, the break of the Tillamook Spit, (also called Bayocean Spit), was so severe the gaping split was one mile wide. Within seconds of the break, the onrushing sea water wiped out the entire oyster farming business in Tillamook Bay.

An example of what can happen when jetties fall into disrepair and dredging is discontinued, was readily seen at the Nehalem Bay entrance. When the jetty project was completed in 1918, there was sufficient lumber and salmon interests to warrant its maintenance. As the years passed, much of the basic industry on the bay declined and with it went government funds for repairing the jetties and dredging the bar channel. Where once commercial lumber schooners and small freight boats crossed, one could almost walk across the entrance at extreme low tide. These jetties, worn almost flat, were rebuilt in the 1980's.

Seagulls can walk across the entrance of the Yachats River but descendants of the pioneers can remember when a 40-foot commercial craft was able to cross the bar.

The Oregon coast attracts millions of visitors annually and

many camp and fish at the numerous parks along the beach several of which are at or near the bar jetties.

The seaward end of any Oregon jetty is often swept by waves that pose a serious danger to trespassers. A single ocean wave can generate a force of 20 tons, therefore woe be to any person atop the jetty when the surf is running high and creaming the rocks.

Bar entrances on the Oregon coast from north to south are:

Columbia River	Siuslaw River
Nehalem Bay	Umpqua River
Tillamook Bay	Coos Bay
Siletz Bay	Coquille River
Depoe Bay	Rogue River
Yaquina Bay	Chetco River
Alsea River	

In the opinion of many commercial fish boat and pleasure craft operators, Tillamook, Umpqua, Coquille or Rogue bars, under rough conditions, are the most dangerous on the coast. □

Sit on a rock at the beach and relax from the daily grind, as Marla Harris, R.N., is doing at the beach north of Cape Blanco.

111

Although Sir Francis Drake declared he met "vile stinking fogge" off the Oregon coast, many of today's coast visitors take the fog in their stride and enjoy the beach anyway.

112

Chapter 9
Semper Paratus
(–Always Ready–)
The Coast Guard

Coast Guard rescue craft are called on to perform some very dangerous tasks especially around bar entrances where the sea and surf always pose a threat to any craft in good or bad weather. These motor lifeboats are designed to roll completely over and return to a righted position. For the men who live through the 360-degree roll, it is a nightmare experience they will never forget. Several of these rescue craft have flipped in Oregon coastal waters usually after getting broadsided by breakers on rescue missions. The swells on the Umpqua bar and its offshore waters are perhaps the most spectacular on the coast.

Following a long and demanding training session in the surf, the crew of the self-bailing, self-righting Coast Guard motor lifeboat *CG-44303* were very tired. Having undergone exercises in some spine-tingling maneuvers through fantastically heavy surf, the new trainees had never dreamed that such wave action existed. It was designed by nature to condition men for the real thing – should an emergency arise.

Exercises over for the day, all hands rejoiced as the boat's coxswain, who was also the officer-in-charge of the station, headed back across the bar to the station and hot showers. The surf had been steadily building and was inundating the jetty rocks. The brisk October breeze excited the waters and as the combers hit shallow bottom they mounted like liquid mountains. The well-experienced skipper was not necessarily concerned as he had experienced the vagaries of the rough bar numerous times. He figured the rougher the swells the better experienced his crew would be for rescue missions. The neophytes, green around the gills, were wondering why they had chosen such duty? Little did they know what was coming.

Mounting far behind the boat's wake was a giant sneaker. Like a seismic wave, it rose suddenly to about 20 feet then without warning cascaded over the fantail of the boat. The startled helmsman tried to gain control by backing down on his engines but the propellers, out of water, fanned only air. Now broadside to the massive swells, the craft began heeling over. Fear masked the faces of the small crew. Towering over them, a great wall of water crashed down with crushing power. In the flashing of an eye, the lifeboat was on her side at 90 degrees. Nothing was left to do but clutch anything solid and then pray.

"Hang on!" shouted the skipper frantically, hoping that all he had taught his crew had soaked in.

Some earlier had a chance to strap themselves into position, but the others had only time to take a stance. The only move the *44303* was going to do was turn completely over. Knees bent for cushioning effect, the men pushed upward with every bit of strength they possessed bracing themselves solidly between the safety grab rails and the deck. Desperately filling their lungs with air, they suddenly felt themselves upside down under the weight of tons of frigid, madly swirling water. Lungs began to burn for want of air and the pressure seemed as if it would crush them.

There was that terrible compulsion to break free rather than follow instructions. Better judgment told them that if they hung on long enough the boat would right itself. Those terrible moments seemed an etemity but hang on they did as their instructor had warned. To let go they risked being chewed by the spinning propellers.

The experience can not be adequately described unless one has gone through such a trial. As the boat rolled, one of the crew was in the cabin and was fortunate enough to have a large air bubble pass over his head allowing him an extra breath. The others had to either wait to breathe or drown. Finally, just as the builders had guaranteed, the boat righted itself

Ironically, the diesel engines kept purring through the entire ordeal. Undamaged, the motor lifeboat continued on to her station her once green crew seemingly, in a few seconds, having aged ten years. They would long remember that training cruise of October

12, 1969.

As for the boat's skipper, a chief petty officer who had pioneered the use of that type of craft, it was the fifth time he had rolled a boat. Before his career ended while at the Yaquina Bay Coast Guard Station, he underwent the experience nine times without any adverse effects. The man was the decorated, professional (cigar-smoking) lifesaver, Chief Petty Officer Tom McAdams. Chief McAdams put in 26½ years of Coast Guard service finally taking his retirement at age 47.

In June of 1977, he was awarded the coveted Coast Guard Legion of Merit Medal for his valuable services and for the saving of scores of lives. His knowledge of motor lifeboats and of surf conditions was considered second to none. He was chosen as a subject for the Charles Kuralt national CBS television program, *Who's Who*. McAdams retired on his beloved Oregon coast and became a commercial fisherman.

McAdams' successor, Chief Daniel Sutherland, while assigned to the Coos Bay Coast Guard Station, helped put an entry in *The Guinness Book of World Records*. This happened while on a 52-foot Coast Guard motor lifeboat – one of only four of her type in the nation at that time. And it happened twice in rough seas on a night in November of 1971.

Said Sutherland:

> It was the only time a 52-foot Coast Guard lifeboat had turned 360-degrees, capsizing and fighting itself in rough seas. It's quite a boat. It'll take you to hell and back if you can hang on.

In June of 1965, a Coast Guard 44-footer struck the south jetty of the Umpqua bar. The craft didn't do a flip, but three men and two women received injuries.

One of the more tragic events in Coast Guard history involved a multiple accident off the Columbia River bar on Jan. 12, 1961. During the attempted rescue of the troubled troller *Mermaid,* three motor lifeboats were lost. These were the 52-foot *Triumph* along with a 40-foot and a 36-foot rescue craft. This mission was costly and made headlines. Five Coast Guardsmen lost their lives and two fishermen also perished.

Modern Coast Guard motor lifeboats and surf boats, foot for foot, are perhaps the best balanced craft afloat.

SANTA CLARA ASHORE COOS BAY REXFIELD PHOTO MARSHFIELD ORE.
12- LIVES LOST

BLUE MAGPIE

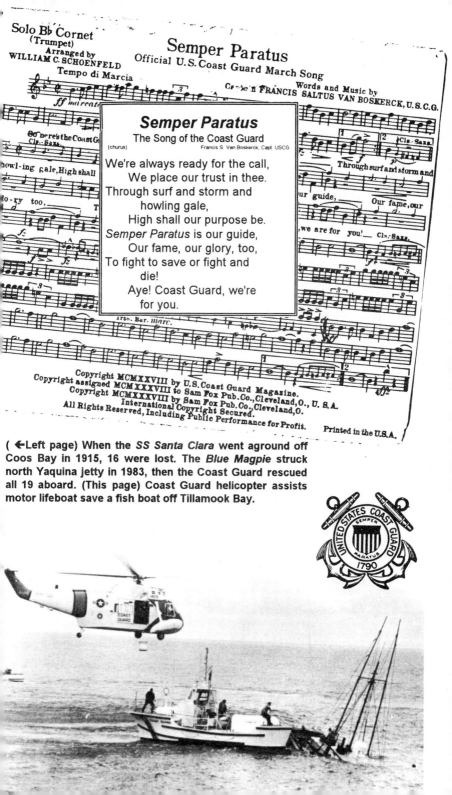

Solo B♭ Cornet
(Trumpet)
Arranged by
WILLIAM C. SCHOENFELD
Tempo di Marcia

Semper Paratus
Official U.S. Coast Guard March Song

Words and Music by
Captain FRANCIS SALTUS VAN BOSKERCK, U.S.C.G.

Semper Paratus
The Song of the Coast Guard
(chorus)   Francis S Van Boskerck, Capt USCG

We're always ready for the call,
   We place our trust in thee.
Through surf and storm and
     howling gale,
   High shall our purpose be.
Semper Paratus is our guide,
   Our fame, our glory, too,
To fight to save or fight and
     die!
   Aye! Coast Guard, we're
     for you.

(←Left page) When the *SS Santa Clara* went aground off
Coos Bay in 1915, 16 were lost. The *Blue Magpie* struck
north Yaquina jetty in 1983, then the Coast Guard rescued
all 19 aboard. (This page) Coast Guard helicopter assists
motor lifeboat save a fish boat off Tillamook Bay.

Boat shown is believed to be one of the first of the long line of 36-foot unsinkable, self-righting motor lifeboats assigned to Cape Disappointment Lifesaving Station in 1920's.

One of the last of the 36-foot motor lifeboats which were replaced by the 44-foot design shown on page 119.

The great expanse of ocean from the Orient to the Pacific Northwest is wide open all the way, leaving nothing on which the waves can snub their noses for nearly 5,000 miles. When they reach the bar entrances along the Oregon Coast following storms, they build to great heights before spilling and expiring on the beach or crashing into headlands.

Cape Disappointment Station, in the lee of the Columbia

Coast Guard "44-boat," CG44303, on practice maneuvers, *top,* in spectacular surf off Umpqua River. *Lower:* Up, Up and over she goes! Search and rescue motor lifeboat plows solidly into a whopper. These craft are self-righting and self-bailing and can survive a 360-degree roll but in so doing is a nightmare experience for the crew.

119

THE UNITED STATES COAST GUARD, and earlier the U. S. Life Saving Service, is responsible for the promotion of safety of life and property on and over the high seas and waters of the United States....

This obligation is met by a force of ships and boats of various sizes and with helicopters and fixed-wing aircraft.

The Coast Guard operates its National Motor Lifeboat School at Cape Disappointment where training takes place in the rugged waters of the Columbia river, on the Columbia River bar, and in the open ocean.

For many decades the Coast Guard, and the life Saving Service before it, has tested new models of boats always seeking the best craft for the unique requirements of the service. At this writing, just completing a rigorous shakedown, is a new 47-foot class Motor Lifeboat headed by a special crew under the MLB Replacement project. The "47-boat," of which there is but a single unit at this time, replaces the earlier "44-boat" of the 1960's. There are improvements in the new craft including a closed, reinforced cabin that makes the boat much safer in heavy seas or when the boat, which is of the unsinkable, self-righting design, rolls over.

The Ultimate plan is to replace the older 44-foot boats over a period of time.

River's north entrance, is the busiest on the west coast. The station provides search and rescue (SAR) for the southern coast of Washinton and the northern coast of Oregon as well as in the Columbia River. Here is located a Search and Rescue Coast Guard station as well as the Motor Lifeboat School. Every member of the Coast Guard who is destined for S&R duty passes through this school.

Not far behind for being busy is the Westport Coast Guard Station at the entrance to Grays Harbor. Then follows the Umpqua River Station at Salmon Harbor on Winchester Bay which logs about 350 assistance calls each year even though it is not in a heavily populated area. The first self-righting 44-foot motor lifeboat was assigned there in 1964. Station personnel have rescued more than 500 persons that might otherwise have drowned. For the most part, the rescue craft cater to distress calls from commercial fishing craft, charter boats and pleasure craft as do most of the other stations today. In the years past before modern innovations in navigation, commercial cargo vessels hugged the Oregon coast with the result that hundreds were wrecked. The men in the shore-based SAR stations of today go out under all conditions just as did the old U. S. Life Saving Service with surf boats propelled by men at oars.

Today, while the motor lifeboats continue to serve, the Coast Guard operates three full-service helicopter-equipped air stations. One is near Astoria. The others are on the south Oregon coast at North Bend and from South Beach near Newport.

Large cargo vessels have mostly replaced the much smaller freighters commonly seen hugging the coast years earlier. These newer vessels have no reason to cruise near the coast due to electronic navigation equipment. Major shipwreck has diminished due mostly to modern marine technology and better safety regulations.

When man is in peril on the sea, the motto of the Coast Guard is recalled:

You have to go out but you don't have to come back.

☐

(Top) During World War II, the U. S. Navy built the Tillamook
Naval Air Station and equipped it with blimps for off-shore anti-
submarine patrols. Blimp shown, hovering over Bayocean
Beach, is recent experimental model. (Lower) Beach at Tierra
del Mar.

Chapter 10
World War II Excitement

In the entire Japanese Navy during World War II no enemy commander harassed the Oregon coast more than did Commander Meiji Tagami, master of the far-ranging Imperial Japanese submarine *I-25*. This dedicated, persistent naval officer gave American Naval and Army officers and soldiers the jitters. He shelled Fort Stevens, sank offshore ships and caused a forest fire in Curry County. Had he been fighting for the allied cause, he would have been highly honored for his daring, cunning aggressiveness.

A B-25B medium bomber crew was decorated for the sinking of what was announced to have been a Japanese submarine off the Oregon coast on Christmas morning of 1941. That submarine was reputedly the *I-25*. But if the sub was sunk, how could skipper Tagami toast writer and publisher Bert Webber in a Tokyo Navy Club reception 34 years later in 1975? The sub's executive officer, Lt. Tatsuo Tsukuduo (later Admiral) recalled, following the war, he supposed Lt. Everett "Brick" Holstrom, the bomber pilot, had merely bombed the sub's bilge oil, which had just been pumped overboard off the Columbia River.

The "sinking" has been the subject of many arguments since the war but one outstanding fact is clear: While nobody can or will identify what it was Brick Holstrom dropped his bombs on, the bombs certainly never hit or sank the *I-25*.

Tagami's navigational skills were exceptional. He did not take risks and after the war an American veteran said to him:

It would have been good to serve with you for you always brought your ship home – except you were fighting on the wrong side. –Bert Webber

Commander Tagami, unlike most of his Naval Academy classmates, survived the war and was well and hearty when the surrender documents were signed aboard the battleship *Missouri* on August 14, 1945.

Nine Japanese submarines departed from Yokosuka Navy Yard in November 1941 destined for the action during the Pearl Harbor raid. With orders to proceed to the U. S. mainland after the bombing in Hawaii, we find by mid-December the *I-25* was off the Columbia River. Then in the spring of 1942, Meiji Tagami, with his submarine, was back again.

As part of the Aleutian Patrol, *I-25,* an aircraft-carrying submarine, launched its plane (E-14Y1 GLEN) for a spy flight over Kodiak. Extending this cruise once more to the Columbia River, the bold Japanese commander ordered his gun crew to shell in the direction of Fort Stevens on the night of June 21, 1942.*

Some of *I-25's* 17 shells fired from the 14cm x 50 cal. (approx. 5½-inch) deck gun whizzed through the darkness, one striking right in front of the 10-inch harbor defense artillery battery. The only damage done, according to members who were there, "They shot hell out of our baseball diamond's backstop."

Excitement was at a high level and nobody slept for the rest of the night. But the Oregon National Guard's 249th Coast Artillery –Harbor Defense – was on the job, and they were ready.

Again in mid-August 1942, the *I-25* with Tagami still in command, departed Yokosuka, with a new twist to the war. Her float plane was specially equipped with bomb racks for incendiary bombs. This series of planned raids were to start forest fires as retaliation for the Doolittle raid on five Japanese cities on April 18, 1942. This was a tit-for-tat matter. The Japanese had raided Pearl Harbor. Lt. Colonel (later General) Doolittle had raided Japan. Now it was the Japanese turn to strike the American

* All of the Japanese trouble-making against Oregon is accounted for in specific detail in *Silent Siege III: Japanese Attacks On North America in WWII; Ships Sunk, Air Raids, Bombs Dropped, Civilians Killed.* See bibliography. There are various writers who err in reporting that Skipper Tagami's shooting of Fort Stevens in June 1942 was the first enemy naval attack on the U. S. mainland since the war of 1812. During the First World War, a German submarine shelled and sank a ship off Long Island, New York and some of the shells also hit the nearby beach. Many writers also report that the *I-25* was out of range of Fort Stevens' guns therefore the fort did not return the fire. Wrong! The Japanese submarine was within range of Battery Russell at all times, but did not know it at the time, according to testimony of Meiji Tagami to Bert Webber in letters and personally at a reception in Tokyo in 1975.

homeland with an air attack and the target was "OREGON."

The plan was not to bomb cities, but to start forest fires that would take American manpower away from shore surveillance and become fire fighters. *I-25* launched its plane at 42° N latitude – right off the Oregon-California line – but about 50 miles at sea. Taking his bearings from Cape Blanco lighthouse, Flight-Warrant officer Nobuo Fujita, with his observer-gunner Shoji Okuda on September 9, 1942 flew inland, above the thick fog and dropped bombs on Wheeler Ridge, a dozen miles east of Brookings.

Because there had been rain for a week, the forests were wet and only one fire was started. The 6 a.m. bombing was not detected until about noon. Then two foresters were dispatched to do whatever was needed to put it out.

The fire fighters, Howard Gardner and Keith V. Johnson (later Admiral USN), were amazed to report by walkie-talkie radio that the bomb fragments had Japanese markings! The furor this caused is treated in the book *Silent Siege-III.*

Again on Sept. 29, the plane was dispatched on another incendiary bombing mission. This flight was up the Sixes River draining area east from Port Orford. Despite close searches through the years, there has never been, to the present writing, any trace of the two 76kg bombs Fujita and Okuda dropped. There were no fires started from these bombs.

The object of these attacks was to burn down the timber industry in the Pacific Northwest. Further attacks were planned, but these had to wait another two years.

America now had its eyes on the Pacific Coast. There had been ship sinkings along the coast from Cape Flattery to near San Diego. The mouth of the Columbia was mined by the Coast Artillery. Immediately after the Pearl Harbor attack, the beaches near the Columbia River, on both the Washington and Oregon sides, were patrolled by Battery B of the 249th Coast Artillery. Eventually, the Coast Guard took over most of the beach patrols.

Lookout towers were spread along the Oregon coast and all lighthouses were ordered to stand 24-hour guard as lookouts for submarines as well as enemy airplanes.

Off the coast, Commander Meiji Tagami was busy looking for targets of opportunity – ships. He didn't have to wait long.

A few days later, a bearing was taken on a ship that turned out to be a tanker, the *Camden,* Captain D. W. Davidson.

There was a light chop from the northwest and in the early morning daylight, visibility was excellent..

The submarine's torpedoes were fired striking the *Camden.* The Swedish motor vessel *Kookaburra* rescued the survivors from the tanker's lifeboats and took them to Port Angeles where they were put ashore.

The day after the attack, the tug *Kenai* spotted the wallowing tanker, got a line aboard and began towing her slowly toward the Columbia River. When off the entrance, the ship was down so low in the water that a bar crossing could not be risked so it was decided to continue the tow to Puget Sound. Off Grays Harbor, the dying vessel suddenly burst into flames then plunged to the bottom in 52 fathoms at position, 46°46'38" N. 124°31'15" W.

Fresh from the kill of the *Camden,* the *I-25* continued her snoop. In another day, the Richfield Oil Company tanker *Larry Doheny,* Captain Olaf Breiland, Portland-bound out of Long Beach with 66,000 barrels of fuel oil was spotted. It was night. The vessel was blacked out and steaming at a steady 10-knots.

At precisely 10:07 p. m. a dull thud shook the *Doheny,* followed by a loud snapping noise. Flames suddenly leaped into the sky. A torpedo struck No. 2 tank on the port side forward ripping out a 12 by 14 foot hole. Within a few minutes the tanker was aflame from stem to stern.

Tagami specifically told Bert Webber he saw no other vessels the night of the *Doheny* attack. But come first light of dawn there was a surprise for the survivors who were in lifeboats. Standing in to them was a ship. People in the various ports where this ship had been seen believed she was just the trampish-looking little lumber freighter *Coos Bay.* *

The ship came alongside to rescue the survivors. In the meantime, the Navy sent ships to search for and depth charge the

---

* The rescue ship was a double-identity vessel. It looked like a freighter but it was a secret U. S. Navy "Q" ship. The mission of a "Q" ship is to purposely get caught, sailing alone, by an enemy sub then when the sub is in close range, the sailors on the ship drop false work and shoot the submarine trying to sink it with 5-inch Naval guns. Four "Q" ships operated in the Atlantic Ocean in WWII but only one, the *Coos Bay/USS Anacapa* worked the Pacific. Pictures of the sinking ships and the *Anacapa* are in *Silent Siege-III.*

I-25. This caused no little bit of apprehension on the submarine. Skipper Tagami, a cool operator under stress, inched his vessel along the bottom of the ocean remaining in silence until the activity cooled down. Where did the submarine settle? On the bottom of the bay offshore from Port Orford!

The *I-25* then left the Oregon coast for the trip, via the great circle route, to Japan. But there is one more intriguing incident for this submarine along the Northwest Coast. This time it was a distance west of Washington state. Kou Maki, the sub's sonar operator, reported picking up the throb of two different ships' engines. Through the periscope, skipper Tagami sighted two submarines which he believed to be American. Using his last torpedo, Kenji Takezawa, the torpedo-man, "mashed the button." He wrote: "The explosion followed in about 20 seconds with damage to *I-25* because of closeness." The undetected Japanese sub suffered a shock from the explosion so severe it *broke all the porcelain toilets*!

The great secret weapons the German's had developed with which they devastated England were the "buzz-bomb" and the V-2 rocket bombs. The Japanese had their secret weapon but on a much different scale. We recall the plan in September of 1942 for Tagami's launching of pilots Fujita and Okuda in a small sub-marine-carried airplane to bomb the forest to start fires in the Pacific Northwest. While this had been just the initial attack, the Imperial Japanese Navy would not allow its subs to do this again because the IJN had lost most of its power in the Battle of Midway and in the Guadalcanal campaign. The High Command told the Japanese Army if it wanted to bomb the American homeland it would have to think up some other way to do it.

Years earlier the Japanese had made comprehensive studies of the upper air currents and determined it was feasible to bomb the American mainland using pilotless high-floating bomb-carrying balloons. To make an amazingly detailed and totally fascinating story short for the purpose of this book, the Japanese built balloons of hand-made paper stuck together with potato paste, filled them with deadly hydrogen, hung bombs under them and launched them into the jet stream.

In all, 45 balloon and bomb landing/explosion incidents are

officially recorded in Oregon, 28 in Washington, 25 in California – over 350 incidents as far east as Detroit, Michigan. Others are as far north as Alaska and some in Mexico.*

Along the Oregon coast, balloon bomb incidents are recorded for :

North Bend	Parkersburg
Coquille	Mt. Neah-kah-Nie

Silence –The Best Defense

Because of a unique understanding between the American government and all the newspaper editors and radio news broadcasters, nobody talked. The Japanese did not learn until after the war that one of these bomb-carrying balloons crashed in Southern Oregon and the explosion killed all the kids and an adult who were on a Sunday School picnic.

The hectic days following Pearl Harbor prompted much action along the Oregon coast. The state's geographical nature, with numerous sandy beaches, made the Oregon coast a likely place for a Japanese invasion.

Immediately after Pearl Harbor, there was a general blackout but it did not start until the next night. Tillamook Rock's beacon continued to burn but Coast guardsmen covered buoy lights.

The blackout was responsible for a major shipwreck near the entrance to the Columbia River. The 420 foot Matson freighter *Mauna Ala,* Captain C. W. Saunders, running at full speed, slammed aground on Clatsop Spit on December 10th.

The ship was called "The Christmas Ship" and had sailed for Hawaii just a few days earlier loaded with Christmas trees from Oregon forests and freezers full of turkeys for holiday meals. With the start of war, the unarmed ship was ordered to reverse course and head for refuge in the Columbia River.

Although the vessel was moving almost at a dead-slow, due to mixed signals in the blackout, the vessel went to full speed for the dash into the river. It missed its invisible mark and piled up on the spit. Probably one of the most forlorn photographs ever made of such a disaster was that of a man, bundled against the cold,

---

* There are several chapters about the *FUGO,* the mysterious "wind-ship weapon" – balloon bombs – in *Silent Siege-III.*

standing holding a dead turkey by the neck. –Merry Christmas Hawaii!

Coast Guard lifeboats removed the crew of 35. There were no casualties.

At the hearing conducted by the Bureau of Inspection and Navigation, the commissioners ruled:

...the blackout of navigational aids, lights, and silencing of radio beacons at the mouth of the Columbia River under wartime restrictions caused the wreck of the *Mauna Ala,* which stranded on Clatsop Spit Dec. 10, 1941."

The vessel, pounded by the fury of a winter storm, could not be salvaged. The ship and the cargo were a total loss.

It is true, but the "politically correct" press has not reported much about it, that before the war started the American Army Signal Corps had cracked the Japanese Diplomatic code. In short, the American government was reading the Japanese' mail to its embassies. There are dozens upon dozens of documented messages wherein Tokyo was lining up its nationals as well as second-generation Japanese born in the United States, to aid the homeland in case of the war. Because of Imperial edict that all Japanese males, regardless of where they were born, were obligated to serve in the Japanese military, there was fear, based on the intelligence gathered from the coded messages, that an invasion of the west coast was in the plans.

To thwart this plausibility, two actions were taken:

1. The coasts of Washington, Oregon and California, and part of Arizona, were declared to be wartime military areas. The order declared that "all persons" considered to be a threat – the Japanese were not named – were to move. This ultimately led to the relocation of Germans, Italians and Japanese away from these military areas. *

2. The U. S. military commanders decided that the threat of invasion was indeed plausible, therefore immediate plans were made to institute a Coast Guard Beach Patrol. The Coast Guard rushed into action and established Sectors of Command on the coasts. In Oregon, there were two Sectors. These were the Astoria

---

* Refer to *American and Japanese Relocation in World War II; Fact, Fiction & Fallacy.* See bibliography.

Sector and the Coos Bay Sector. The Astoria region included areas in Washington from Cape Elizabeth to the Columbia River then in Oregon south to Cascade Head. There were Coast Guard Beach Patrol Detachments assigned at:

Seaside	Bayocean
Cannon Beach	Netarts
Rockaway Beach	Pacific City

In the Coos Bay Section, Beach Patrol Detachments were stationed at:

Taft	Agate Beach
Depoe Bay	Coquille River
Yaquina Bay	Floras Lake
Waldport	Cape Blanco
Heceta Head	Port Orford
Siuslaw River	Euchre Creek
Umpqua River	Rogue River
Saunders Lake	Pistol River
Coos Bay	Brookings

The most vulnerable and most isolated length of beach was declared to be from Port Orford to Bandon along the south Oregon Coast. Accordingly, a very large Detachment of some 85 men were assigned to the Floras Lake Beach Patrol. This site was at the ghost town of Lakeport, a real estate scam around 1910-1915. A comprehensive account, with many pictures of the beach patrol units activities is found in *Lakeport; Ghost Town of the South Oregon Coast.* (See bibliography). The Coast Guard at Floras Lake had a boat, radios, pistols, rifles as well as at least one machine gun plus a number of attack dogs.

Other detachments also had war dogs and many had horses. All beaches were searched around the clock by the Coast Guard (except for Clatsop Spit which was monitored by the 249th Coast Artillery soldiers).

The author, having enlisted in the Coast Guard, was involved in an incident that caused a great amount of concern at the time. The experience is recalled:

The place was Tierra del Mar Beach, north of Pacific City, where there was a detachment of Coast Guardsmen. Due to strictly enforced restrictions, all communications with headquarters were in code. On a routine night patrol we were burdened down with the usual equipment: rifles, sidearms, walkie-talkie and a patrol dog. To protect the innocent, we will refer to my partner as Joe.

It was a late fall evening and the truck left us at a wilderness spot from where we had to walk about a mile to the beach. The trail ended at a high bank from which a switch back path led down to the sand where our long trek would begin.

All across the nation appeals had gone out for dog owners to donate their pets for the war effort. Demand was generally for German shepherds, Doberman pinschers and similar breeds that could be properly trained for patrol and attack purposes. So much in demand were the canines that the quotas could not be filled. Thus, the restrictions as to types of breeds were relaxed and in certain cases dogs of the hunting variety were accepted. Most of the animals assigned to Pacific City were proper types, but somehow a pointer had slipped in and out of the K-9 Corps training school. How this dog graduated remains one of the great mysteries of the war but there he was, big as life and twice as stupid. It took little knowledge to know that hunting dogs made extremely poor war dogs because their noses concentrated on the scent of birds and animals, instead of humans.

Such a dog was "Pluto," properly named for his Disney double. Always the last to be assigned to a patrol unit because he had an insatiable instinct to forget his training and take-off whenever there was a bird to be pursued. If, when a bird swooped by, a Coast Guardsman happened to be on the other end of the leash, it was tantamount to being astride a spooked horse.

It was dusk. Below the cliff lay six miles of beach we were assigned to patrol. Suddenly the dog caught sight of a flock of sandpipers swooping along the ridge and he was off to the races with me on the other end. The strength of that canine was unbelievable and it took about 15 minutes to get him partially calmed down. The two of us decided that perhaps if we let him loose for a few minutes he would run his legs off and settle down for the long patrol ahead of us. That was a mistake.

We violated the rule and set him free. Like an express train, this dog with tongue hanging around his knees, roared off to the chase. Each time the sandpipers reversed flight so did he. For some reason that evening there was a great number of seabirds flying along the crest of the 60 foot bank.

The sandpipers seemed to know they were dealing with a dumb brute who couldn't get out of his own way. Suddenly Pluto stopped. Panting furiously, he leaned far out over the cliff just as a sharp gust of wind caught his rump and over the bank he went.

We scurried down to the beach and the two of us took different directions looking for our so-called peculiar war dog.

"Over here!" I shouted to Joe.

At first we thought Pluto was dead having made a nose-dive into the sand.

What to do now? We were to have walked the six miles of beach then be picked up by the midnight relief truck. We decided to use the radio. But we couldn't blurt out that while off-leash and chasing birds, our deadly attack war dog had fallen off a cliff.

Joe sat down by a large piece of driftwood and with shielded flashlight, looked through the code book for a suitable message. Joe found a concise statement that seemed to handle the matter: 'Patrolman injured.'

He sent the message. There was no answer.

'They won't confirm,' declared Joe as he pulled the earphones from his head.

Being that the dog was out cold, we had to make a stretcher so we used pieces of driftwood on which to drag the dog behind us.

Some time later, with night falling, after we'd looked at our semi-conscious and bleeding dog, Joe found a whiskey bottle in the sand that had a drag left in it. We decided it might revive the dog so we poured what was left in the bottle down his throat. Pluto gave a jerk, gulped once then seemed to settle down for a nap.

Suddenly Joe exclaimed, 'Did you hear that?'

'What?' I asked.

'Listen! It sounds like soldiers walking through the sand.

'Sure does,' I whispered, hand cupped to my ears. 'Sounds more like a whole regiment.'

We ran and hid behind a pile of driftwood fully believing a full scale Japanese invasion was in progress.

Then: 'Halt! Who goes there? Stand and identify yourselves!' –came from a hoarse voice from out in the dark.

As we rose slowly from our prone position, what seemed like a brilliant searchlight blinded our eyes. Out stepped a high-ranking Army officer flanked on all sides by a vast contingent of soldiers. Representatives from all three branches of the service had flooded our immediate area and none of them were Japanese.

After meekly identifying ourselves, the spokesman bellowed, 'Your code message, PATROLMAN INJURED.' Where are the invaders? –the extent of your injuries?'

Our communication was taken to have meant an invasion, or at least some kind of enemy action in which injuries had been sustained by men. A red alert had gone out and battle-ready troops most of whom had been roused from sleep had converged at the rendezvous point.

Joe and I looked at each other then we presented Pluto, in his stupor, to these 'authorities.' Reviving momentarily, the dog managed a large belch and then fell back to sleep.

When our account of this incident passed through the troops I thought we would be tarred and feathered on the spot. Oaths and cursing filled the cool Oregon beach night air.

There was dead silence in the truck all the way back to Pacific City. While the dog went to the veterinarian, the two of us went before the commanding officer. Among other discipline, we had our duty changed from Beach Patrolmen to weeks of peeling spuds.

132

Because of strict war secrecy, the story remained hushed and never made the newspapers. In fact, it did not appear in the official Coast Guard Beach Patrol Daily War Diary.

As for Pluto, he recovered but his further services were advisedly limited. □

The British bark *Peter Iredale* went ashore and stayed there in 1906. Four kids, Richard, Marymerle (with dog), Lauren and Dale Webber tried to straighten the hulk's attitude in this mid-1960's view. During World War II, Battery B of the 249th Coast Artillery (Harbor Defense), did guard duty on this beach – often used the *Iredale* for target practice. Little is left of the landmark today. Find it near Fort Stevens State Park. Look for signs. For view of the ship in 1906, turn the page.

Remains of British bark *Peter Iredale*, popular visitor attraction (top), has been a landmark on the Oregon coast since it went aground on October 25, 1906. (Lower) The Astor Column in Astoria, 125 feet tall, has spiral stairs to the top.

Chapter 11
Parks, Lighthouses and Beachcombing
Includes Selected Other Places of Interest
Compiled by Margie Webber, co-author: *I'd Rather Be Beachcombing*

The state parks along the Oregon Coast, and the historical lighthouses, draw thousands upon thousands of campers and visitors every year and the numbers keep increasing. Is it the climate? Is it the historical museums? Is it the view? We'll propose one of the reasons is the fantastic beachcombing.*

For our purposes, we list the parks and lighthouses starting with those in the north and continuing to the southern border. It is recommended that a current edition of the Official Oregon State Highway Map be consulted for locations and beach access routes.

Recalling that all Oregon beaches are public highways, it is urgent that drivers consult the highway map to determine open and closed dates for motor vehicles on beaches. Several years ago it became necessary, for public safety, due to high number of pedestrians on the most popular beaches, to publish the dates beaches are open to motor vehicles.

Safety tips: The speed limit on the beaches is 25 mph. Those who drive on the sand are generally courting the opportunity to get stuck. It can be costly to hire a tow. Beware of leaving valuables in vehicles.

About these parks:
Some of the facilities listed are operated by Oregon State Park personnel and others by volunteer groups. Days and hours of operation may change without notice. Fees are charged to enter and use some parks, others are free. If there are fees, these should be posted at park entrances. As the State continues acquiring new land for park purposes, the compiler can make no claim for completeness or accuracy.

---

* Refer to *I'd Rather Be Beachcombing*. See bibliography.

The great anchor is exhibited at the Columbia River Maritime Museum in Astoria.

136

Cannon Beach and Haystack Rock, north Oregon coast. Scene is during low tide in summer.

Fort Stevens SP.
Frontage on Columbia River as well as the Pacific Ocean. Lakes, sandy areas, forests. Picnic. This is nearest camping park to the mouth of the Columbia River and Clatsop Beach. Remains of *Peter Iredale* ship that stranded here in 1906. Beachcombing/floats. View. Photography. Historical Area with its remarkable Military Museum; book shop. Drive or hike to Battery Russell, the World War II artillery position that wanted to fire during the Japanese Navy attack on the fort in June 1942 but couldn't get an OK to do so. Refer to *Silent Siege III: Japanese Attacks On North America in WWII; Ships Sunk, Air raids, Bombs Dropped, Civilians Killed.* See bibliography.

Del Ray Beach State Wayside
Hiking. Beachcombing/floats. View. Photography.

Gearhart Ocean Wayside
At mouth of Necanicum River and extending 2 miles to the north. Not developed. Beachcombing/floats. View. Photography.

Ecola SP
At north end of City of Cannon Beach. Steep terrain, dense forest. Hike or drive to Indian Beach. Old growth Sitka spruce. Indian shell middens. Includes 6-mile Tillamook Head Trail. Best views of abandoned Tillamook Rock lighthouse. Artists and photographers frequent here. Refer to *Terrible Tilly; Tillamook Rock Lighthouse; A Biography of a Lighthouse* See also: *Oregon's Seacoast Lighthouses.* See bibliography.

Oriental fishnet floats in many sizes and shapes, mostly Japanese, land along the coasts of Washington and Oregon with consistency in winter months during severe storms.

About Beachcombing For Glass Fishing Floats.
There are lots out there waiting to come in.

The accepted "rule" is never go alone but be on the beach during a severe winter storm, at high tide, when the wind has been blowing at minimum 17 knots from the west or northwest for a number of hours. Between 10 p.m. and 5 a.m. seem best because there are fewer beachcombers racing for the floats as they land with the tide. The key is to acknowledge that the Davidson Current, that runs from south-to-north in winter months, helps floats land. While floats land sometimes in summer months, the odds seem best in winter time.

—*I'd Rather Be Beachcombing*

Haystack Rock, Cannon Beach at minus tide.

Tolovana Beach SP
Provides beach access in midst of community of Tolovana Park. Haystack Rock. Beachcombing/floats. View. Photography.

Arcadia Beach State Wayside
Provides beach access. Forest. Beachcombing/floats. View. Photography.

Hug Point SP
This is a strip of land between Hwy 101 and the ocean at the southern end of City of Cannon Beach. In the days before the highway, vehicles could not get past the point except at low tide so a single-car wide roadway was blasted in the rock just above the beach. The parking and picnicking areas were once a grassy plot on which there were several musty and romantic rental cabins. Trail to small beach. Beachcombing/floats. View. Photography.

Oswald West SP
Hwy 101 runs through center of park earlier called Short Sands Beach SP. Most of Mt. Neah-kah-nie (elev. 1,795 ft) is in the park. Sitka spruce, hemlock, Douglas fir, Western red cedar. Trail. Spectacular view from summit. Camping and picnic areas. Named for Gov. Oswald West in recognition of his 1913 legislation setting aside entire length of Oregon's shore for public use with ownership vested in the State. Four mile shoreline includes Smugglers Cove but no smugglers known to have been there. Cape Falcon, Short Sands Beach. Hiking. View. Photography.

This cannon and capstan came from the U.S. sloop *Shark* which, on September 10, 1846, was wrecked on crossing the Columbia River bar. These pieces, attached to a section of deck, washed ashore and the beach was named Cannon Beach. These relics are now at Clatsop County Museum in Astoria.

Nehalem Bay SP

Entire length of 3-mile long wind-swept Nehalem Spit. Horse camp, corrals, 7.5 miles equestrian trail, 1.5 mile bike trail. Airport fly-in camp. Camping; picnic. Carry water and snack if hiking to end as walking is slow in sand. Watch for pieces of historic beeswax. Beachcombing/floats. View. Photography.

Manhattan Beach SP

Public parking and beach access. Beachcombing/floats - little driftwood. View. Photography.

Rockaway Beach SP

Public parking and beach access. Picnic. Beachcoming/floats. View. Photography.

Twin Rocks State Wayside

Provides beach access. Undeveloped. Tideland and small beach with offshore rocks called "Twin Rocks." View. Photography.

Tillamook Cheese Factory   Hwy 101 north of Tillamook.

Oregon's largest cheese kitchen. Tours. Book shop.

Tillamook Pioneer Museum   2106 Second St., Tillamook

Special collections include Bayocean (on Tillamook Spit) the town that fell into the sea due to coastal erosion. (Refer to *Bayocean, The Oregon Town That Fell Into the Sea)*; B-17 bomber crash on Cape Lookout during WWII, (refer to *Silent Siege III: Japanese Attacks On North America in WWII)*; natural hist.; military, Naval Air Station; rocks/minerals; beeswax. Book shop.

Tunnel, through Maxwell Point at village of Oceanside, was access to excellent beachcombing north of the point. Rock cave-in closed tunnel several times. Due to risk to visitors, the tunnel was not again reopened. Access to the quaint north beach is presently only at low tide by walking on the sand around the point.

141

Cape Meares SP

National wildlife refuge. Spectacular ocean headland, Sitka spruce and hemlock. For colorful life of historic Cape Meares Lighthouse refer to *Oregon's Seacoast Lighthouses*. See bibliography. The spruce "Octopus Tree" is here. This and lighthouse are highlights of this non-beach access park. Picnic. Hiker-biker camp. Tours; seasonal book shop. View. Photography.

Oceanside Beach State Wayside

In City of Oceanside. Includes Maxwell Point. City beach always a good place for finding glass fishing floats in winter. There is a tunnel through Maxwell point to another beach to the north but due to alleged misuse, by undesirable elements, it was closed denying access to the "north" beach. Beachcombing. View. Photography.

Cape Lookout SP

Encompasses all of Netarts Spit. Rugged, rain forest of Sitka spruce, hemlock, shore pine on ocean headland that reaches 2-miles (trail) to the ocean. View from high, rocky cliffs. About 154 species of birds. Camping, picnic at base of spit. On trail see monument to crew of B-17 bomber that crashed there in 1943. Remnants of plane in undergrowth. This spectacular crash is in *Silent Siege III: Japanese Attacks On North America in WWII*. See bibliography. Erosion in recent years knocked through tall dune, threatened camping area. Damage shown in *Bayocean, The Oregon Town That Fell Into the Sea*. See bibliography. Beachcombing/floats. View. Photography.

Tierra del Mar   Residential area north of Cape Kiwanda

Access to beach on public street. Avoid private property. Long, wide flat beach. Beachcombing/floats - some driftwood. View. Photography.

Cape Kiwanda SP

Bold headland, Cape Kiwanda, looms at north edge of beach and extends about ¼-mile into ocean. Wave-sculpted sandstone cliffs; unique dory launching from beach directly into ocean; (parking on beach for boat trailers); tide pools; dunes. Haystack Rock about ¾-mile offshore. Beachcombing/float-finding area extends for about 1-mile south of park to Pacific City then continues – see Bob Straub SP. View. Photography.

Bob Straub SP (aka Robert Straub SP)

Earlier named Nestucca Sand Spit SP. Includes all of spit to mouth of Nestucca Bay where erosion broke through near its end in 1978. For pictures and details see *Bayocean, The Oregon Town That Fell Into the Sea*. See bibliography. Fly-in at adjacent Pacific City State Airport. Beachcombing /floats - little driftwood. View. Photography.

Neskowin Beach State Wayside

Provides access to "Proposal Rock" at mouth of Neskowin Creek at beach. About 1900 a man proposed to a young lady here thus the name. Trail from parking to beach. Beachcombing/floats - some driftwood View. Photography.

(Top) Beach at Seaside on late August evening. Note "turn-around" which is the western end of U. S. Highway 30. See picture on page 10 for a winter view. Tillamook Head in rear. (Lower) This binary (double) Japanese glass fishnet float came ashore near here. Double floats are considered rare by serious float collectors.

Roads End Beach State Wayside

Provides access to beach by trail. Beachcombing south of park. View. Photography.

143

Driving on the beach can be fun but the risk of becoming stuck in the sand is very great and can be costly. (Lower) Salishan – Siletz Spit–beach is great for beachcombing and hiking. The spit has been over-washed during severe winter storms with risk to the expensive houses one of which has been washed away. Lincoln City in background.

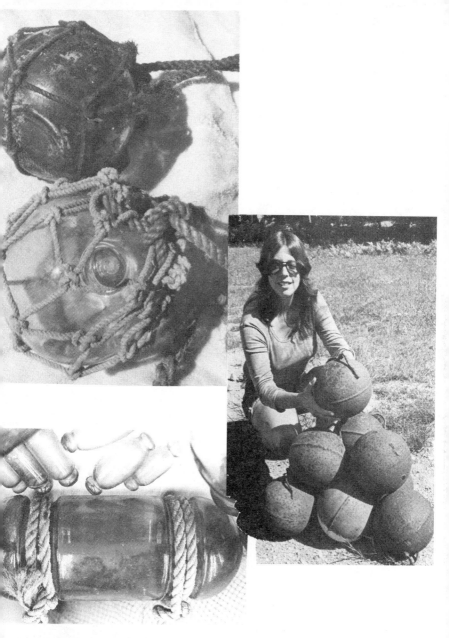

Fishing floats come in many sizes, shapes, materials and from a large number of nations. Most common are Japanese balls (page 138, 143) American Duraglass (top left); Japanese "rolling pins" lower. At right are Russian 8-inch cast iron balls that came in heavily in late 1960's.

145

From time-to-time businesses along the coast exhibit beach findings in their windows. (Top) in a restaurant at Winchester Bay. (Lower) Japanese flask found after a winter storm.

Lots of folks wade and swim in the surf along Oregon's beaches but the water here, the latitudes are in the mid-40's, is always cold.

D River State Wayside

Parking at beach access on D River the shortest river in the world – about 100-yards long. Long, sandy beach subject to erosion during winter storms. View. Beachcombing/floats; driftwood. Photography all year especially during severe, dangerous, winter storms that can throw drift logs onto parking lot and highway.

Devil's Lake SP

In Lincoln City on Hwy 101 on Devil's Lake. Camping includes hiker-biker sites. Tide pools. Photography. (For boating / picnic see East Devil's Lake SP)

East Devil's Lake SP

Picnic area and boat access to lake on east side of Devil's Lake. Photography.

Gleneden Beach State Wayside

Access from Hwy 101 to beach as there is no public access through the Salishan private estates (locked gate) on the Siletz (Salishan) Spit. Long hike to end of spit. Carry water, snack. This entire spit is subject to severe winter erosion during storms. One house has fallen into the ocean. The brand new yacht *Marjean* stranded here in storm is buried on the beach. For stories and many pictures refer to *Bayocean, The Oregon Town That Fell Into the Sea*. See bibliography. Beachcombing/floats; driftwood. View. Photography.

Fogarty Creek SP

Both sides of Hwy 101. Once logged, now supports second-growth Sitka spruce, hemlock, shore pine, alder. Picnic. On beach side, annual sand castle contest. Beachcombing/floats. View. Photography

147

Fogarty Creek State Park showing an incoming tide. In "quiet" summer weather, high tides are not all that high. But there is undertow on most of Oregon's beaches. Photograph made in August.

Boiler Bay State Wayside

Steep, jagged rocky bluff. Spectacular wave action on incoming tide but the boiler from wreck of the *J. Marhoffer*, for which the park is named, seen at low tide. Story of ship's loss is in *Oregon's Seacoast Lighthouses*. See bibliography. View. Photography.

Rocky Creek State Wayside

Park hooded by steep walled forested bluff between Rocky Creek and Whale Cove. Superb view of turbulent wave action against rocky shore on incoming tide. View, photography.

Otter Crest State Wayside

At crest of Cape Foulweather (elev. 453 ft.). Next to the park property is Lookout Observatory and book shop. Often windy. Magnificent view. Photography.

Devil's Punch Bowl SP

Severe wave action roaring in and out of tunnels during incoming tides cause roaring, thundering, reverberating sounds. "Sounds like the Devil stirring his pot." On north side marine garden visible at low tide. On south is wide and long beach. Picnic. Beachcombing/floats. View. Photography.

The famous boiler in Boiler Bay can be walked to at low ride; is totally covered on high tides.

Beverly Beach SP

Favorite coastal overnight camp ground protected from fierce ocean winds. Much of original Sitka spruce and other species logged earlier, second growth trees have excelled. Access to beach from park under highway overpass. Picnic. Beachcombing/floats. View. Photography.

Agate Beach State Wayside

At mouth of Big Creek on beach. Parking for access to beach and agate beds. Beachcombing/agates, floats

Yaquina Head Lighthouse

Operating lighthouse opens to public 1994 with BLM supervision which is building reception area. Watch for new Hwy signs north of Newport. Refer to *Oregon's Seacoast Lighthouses* and to *Yaquina Lighthouses on the Oregon Coast*. See bibliography. Bird and sea-life sanctuary; interpretative exhibits. View. Photography.

Yaquina Bay SP

Overlooks Yaquina Bay and jetties to west extending into ocean – Yaquina Bay Bridge (1936) to southeast. Feature is historic Yaquina Bay Lighthouse that operated only 3 years (1851-1854) now fully restored. Lighthouse noted for its ghosts. Tours. Definitive history of the lighthouse, grounds, in *Yaquina Lighthouses on the Oregon Coast* and in *Oregon's Seacoast Lighthouses*.. See bibliography. Park and overlook open all year. Lighthouse open summers and winter weekends. Book shop. View. Photography.

Starfish are in many Oregon coast tidepools. They are great to look at, slimy to hold, and disturbing them is contrary to law.

South Beach SP
Earlier known as South Beach Wayside and South Newport State Park, were combined into present facility. Sitka spruce and shore pines. Picnic. Dunes. Provides access to beach and south jetty area. Major camping park in Newport area close to Agate Beach, Yaquina Bay Lighthouse, Yaquina Head Lighthouse, Hatfield Marine Science Center and Oregon Coast Aquarium. View. Photography.

Lost Creek SP
Opened for beach access. Includes some of old railroad right-of-way in area of Sitka spruce and shore pine. Picnic. View. Photography.

Ona Beach SP
On both sides of estuary of Beaver Creek. Excellent unusual, attractive forested land developed into fine picnic and restful area at Hwy. Long, broad flat beach. Beachcombing/floats, driftwood. Photography.

Seal Rock State Wayside
Large basaltic rocks ("Castle," "Tourist," "Elephant") offshore are habitats for seals, sea lions, birds. Marine garden seen at low tide in pools. Trail to beach. Excellent beach welcomes glass fishing floats particularly during mid-winter storms. Panoramic view of ocean, offshore rocks. View. Photography.

Driftwood Beach State Wayside
Provides access to beach. Shore pines. Picnic. Beachcombing/floats, driftwood. View. Photography.

150

Driftwood is plentiful along the Oregon coast from about Siletz Bay south. Some collectors make many artistic items and a number are sold in beachside gift shops. (Top) A wag called this "Howard Hughes last portrait" to which the youngster, startled, (lower) seeing it yelled "Mom"!

Governor Patterson Memorial SP

Offers beach access; picnic. Gov. Isaac L. Patterson was first governor to appoint a Park Commission. Forest; long, wide, beach. Beachcombing/floats, driftwood. Photography.

Beachside SP

Earlier called Big Creek SP. Camping. Picnic. Provides access to beach at Big Creek. Wind-swept shore pine.

W. B. Nelson SP

On Eckman Slough east of Waldport. Picnic; swimming; Sitka spruce forest.

Smelt Sands State Wayside

Provides access to beach mostly for smelt fishing. Hiking trail.

Surf fishing is a popular sport along the Oregon coast but how these fellows keep from tangling their lines is anyone's guess.

Yachats Ocean Road State Wayside
Access on south side of Yachats River– tide lands at Yachats estuary – to beach. Panoramic view of ocean, rocks. View. Photography.

Yachats SP
This rocky park offers access to fishing area and protects fish spawning along beach. View. Photography.

Cleft of the Rock Lighthouse
No public access. This privately owned, officially approved lighthouse south of Yachats was activated in 1976, is in shadow of Cape Perpetua (the cape 800 ft. elev. at shore and 1,000 ft elev. 8/10ths mile back – highest on Oregon coast). One of only two lighthouses on Oregon coast showing white and red beams (other is Umpqua River lighthouse). Not open to public. Complete description and pictures in *Oregon's Seacoast Lighthouses.* See Bibliography.

Neptune SP
Irregular stretch (2½ miles) of coastline of rugged, craggy rock ledges, precipitous cliffs against which old King Neptune crashes his fury of huge, frothy-white waves almost at regular intervals during winter storm season. View. Photography.

Scuba diver James Seeley White does "underwater beachcombing" searching for "whatever looks good." Among other things, he has been on the lookout for artifacts from Spanish galleons.

Stonefield Beach State Wayside
Provides access at Ten Mile Creek over a flat grassland that reaches to the beach and mouth of the creek. Beachcombing.

Muriel O. Ponser Memorial State Wayside
This 2-acre tract at mouth of China Creek is where Chinese are alleged to have mined for gold thus the name of the creek. Wind-swept Sitka spruce, shore pine. Beachcombing/floats, driftwood. View. Photography.

Carl G. Washburne Memorial SP
Camping. Picnic. Dense forest of shore pine and Sitka spruce along China Creek with mile-long beach. Tide pools, frequent visit by elk. Heavy coast huckleberry, agate beds, beachcombing/floats. View. Photography

Out-of-area visitors should refer to the current official Oregon state road map for codes showing which beaches are open to motor vehicles.

Devil's Elbow SP

Spectacular ocean cove over which is historic deck arch bridge leading to tunnel. Trail to historic Heceta Head Lighthouse. This rugged area is probably the most photographed scene on the Oregon coast. Sitka spruce, shore pine trees. View. Artists and photographers haunt this park..

Darlingtonia State Wayside

Outstanding feature are the bog-loving carnivorous "Cobra" pitcher-plants that "eat" flies, bugs of all kinds having been attracted by the plants weird odor. Rhododendrons. Close-up photography.

Jessie M. Honneyman Memorial SP

On shores of Woahink Lake (36 ft elev.) and Cleawox Lake (72 ft. elev.) and Pacific Ocean. Heavy forests, water lilies. Camping, picnic, swimming. Sand dunes (joins Oregon Dunes National Recreation Area). Hike to beach. Beach-combing. View. Photography.

Oregon Dunes National Recreation Area

Sand dunes. Trails. Beachcombing/floats, driftwood. View. Photography

Bolon Island Tideways State Wayside

In Umpqua River north of Reedsport. Limited parking. Steep timberland. Trail to top of hill. View. Photography.

154

Attire for a day's serious beachcombing at Bayocean on Tillamook Spit called for long-Johns, a "Typhoon Suit" and gloves because it was a blustery day. Bert Webber's gunny sack will carry whatever is found that is worthy of a 2-mile hike back to the car. There was once a town here but it washed into the sea. The story is in *Bayocean, The Oregon Town That Fell Into the Sea.* (See bibliography)

Umpqua Lighthouse SP
Camping. Picnic. Historic lighthouse, Lake Marie in midst of Douglas fir, Sitka spruce, Western red cedar, giant rhododendrons, elephantine sand dunes (545 ft. elev.). Historic Umpqua lighthouse is one of only two lighthouses on Oregon coast emitting white and red beams – excellent site at night for telling ghost stories as the beam swishes with reflection from nearby trees. (The other white-red flasher is Cleft of the Rock Lighthouse -private- at Cape Perpetua). Earlier lighthouse collapsed as it was built on sand. Refer to *Oregon's Seacoast Lighthouses.* See bibliography. View. Beachcombing /floats, driftwood;

William M. Tugman SP
Camping on Eel Lake. Picnic. Boating, swimming.

Conde B. McCullough Bridgehead State Wayside
On old Hwy north of McCullough Memorial Bridge over Coos Bay. Named for bridge designer. Forested in Sitka spruce. Undeveloped other than boat access.

Cape Arago Lighthouse
Operating historic lighthouse closed to visitors at this writing. For history see *Oregon's Seacoast Lighthouses.* See bibliography. This is third lighthouse here due to erosion. View. Photography.

155

Sea-beaten piece of drift log left high on a beach during a winter storm. The wind was sharp on this clear winter day causing top sand to race across the beach.

Sunset Bay SP
South of Cape Arago Lighthouse. Camping in pine, Sitka spruce, hemlock trees on wind-protected cove with precipitous sandstone bluffs at beach packed hard by tides. Swimming in surf. Hiking. View. Artists and photographers like this park.

Shore Acres SP
Joins Cape Arago SP. Spectacular stretch of ocean shore line once the estate of Louis and Lela Simpson in 1942 with a 3-story manor (15 bedrooms) used by Coast Guard Beach Patrol in WWII (*see* Chapter 10) It was razed in 1948 due to deterioration. The renowned and unusual botanical gardens remain. Spectacular bluff about 40-50 ft high is site for amazing wave action and high spray – as much as 50 ft high – with accompanying roar of incoming tides. Photographers, artists paradise.

Cape Arago SP
At end of Hwy 240. Commanding view of coastline from point about 200-ft above ocean. Offshore rocks. View. Photography.

Seven Devils State Wayside
On exciting, winding county road (Seven Devils Hwy) facing ocean at mouth of Two Mile Creek. Picnics. View. Beachcombing. Photography.

The Dunes National Recreation Area is an amazing place to visit and to enjoy. Its headquarters in Reedsport has maps and directions.

Bullards Beach SP

Forested camping along Coquille River estuary. Picnic. Trails. Park includes Coquille River historic lighthouse also called "Bandon Lighthouse." Refer to *Oregon's Seacoast Lighthouses*. See bibliography. In winter storms, jetties often totally over-swept by crashing incoming tide with beach noted for heavy wave scouring where one day the beach is littered with large logs and driftwood that disappears a few days later. Recently, a winter storm totally covered parking area with heavy logs forcing the beach end of the park to be closed. View. Beachcombing/floats, driftwood. Photography. <u>Note:</u> In winter, best viewpoint for seeing storm-washed jetties is from base of south jetty in City of Bandon.

Bandon Ocean Wayside

Spectacular tideland with exceptionally fine beach. Picnic but no drinking water. Beachcombing/floats, driftwood. View of offshore rocks. Photography.

Bandon SP

Beach with a foredune that shelters nearly 20 acres from rough northwest winds. Picnic. Trails. No drinking water. View. Beachcombing/floats, driftwood. Photography.

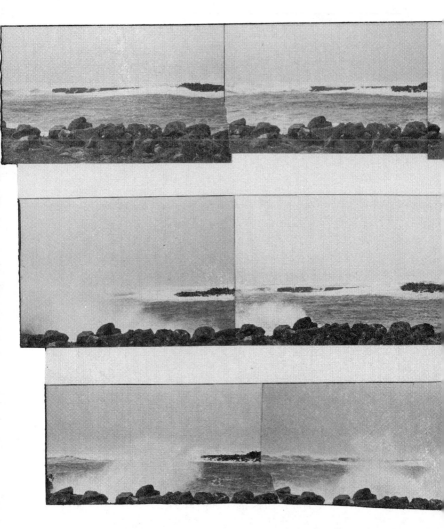

A writer declared that to appreciate the Oregon coast, one should visit in the dead of winter during a high tide and a severe storm and if camping in a trailer, the din on the roof would be like being inside a snare drum during a Sousa march. Camera operators for these pictures were in a camper parked close to base of south jetty. Conditions: High tide, severe wind and rain gusts. Cameraman leaned elbows on steering wheel, squeezed camera shutter between single-swipes of windshield wiper operated manually by assistant. The scene *(Upper left across both pages to*

lower right): Huge breakers, one after another, off end of
north jetty, build, crash, cover, sweep along top of jetty
while south end of same breakers hit south jetty but stay in
channel—crash against side of jetty sending heavy spray
splattering the vehicle. Not a day to be walking on these
jetties. This is wild. This is exciting. This is the stormy,
North Pacific Ocean in all its glory and rage in which ships
are wrecked and sometimes people are lost.

On the beach immediately north of Cape Blanco where spectacular off-shore rocks intrigue beachcombers and photographers.

Boice-Cope County Park

West of Langlois. On northeast corner Floras Lake. Camping. Picnic. Termed best lake in Oregon for wind-surfing. Park is on site of town of Lakeport, largest town in Curry County between 1910-1915 (historical marker). Plan was to dig canal between lake and ocean converting lake into a seaport. But lake is higher than ocean therefore if canal was dug the lake would drain – a real estate scam – so the town failed. Spectacular wreck and salvage of cargo from ship *Bawnmore* that stranded immediately west of lake. Major WWII Coast Guard Beach Patrol station here on alert for threatened Japanese invasion. Fascinating history with pictures in *Lakeport; Ghost Town On the South Oregon Coast.* See bibliography. Trail crosses New River to beach. Beachcombing /floats, driftwood. Photography.

Floras Lake SP

South edge of Floras Lake on ocean. Earlier known as Newburgh SP. Not developed but has colorful history. Sandstone Bluffs north from Blacklock Point was site of quarrying of sand-stone in 1880s shipped to San Francisco for buildings. With no dock possible due to rough surf, pully-line hauling the slabs directly to the ships proved unfeasible so the project collapsed. In WWII Navy built major emergency airport which is today's Curry County Airport. Area covered with ususual plants, dwarfed Sitka spruce, shore pine, rhododendrons, California laurel (also called "myrtlewood"). See Boice-Cope County Park.

Hughes House   Cape Blanco Rd.

On right side of road leading to end of cape. Built in 1898, restored house open in summer by Friends of Cape Blanco. Museum. Tours. Book shop.

160

Beachcombers on the sand just to south of Cape Blanco as the
fog starts to roll in.
(Lower) Lone Ranch Beach on the south Oregon Coast.

161

Cape Blanco Lighthouse

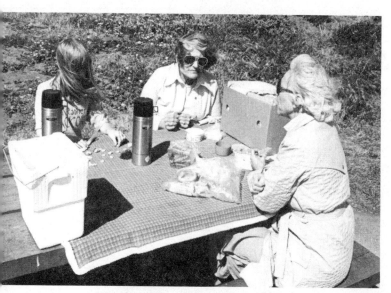

Visitors from South Carolina with Margie Webber, center, on a windy summer day at Ophir Rest Area. During winter storm (lower) there are no picnickers.

Cape Blanco SP

Attractive, wind-swept camping. Trails to north and south beaches. Historic Cape Blanco Lighthouse (headland 245 ft elev. – 42°50'N 124°34'W) farthest westerly point in Oregon. View. Photography.

Paradise Point State Wayside

Access to beach. Beachcombing/floats, driftwood. View. Photography.

(Top) Sunset on the south Oregon coast.
(Lower) Just after dawn on the south Oregon coast.
Pictures made in February 1994 at Hunter Creek.

This view of historic bridge near mouth of Rogue River was photographed in February 1994. Another view of this bridge is on page 101.

Port Orford Heads State Wayside
Ocean bluff location faces bay front on Nellis Cove where old USCG lifeboat station was located. Marine gardens; archaeological area. View. Photography.

Battle Rock Park
Former State Park presently administered by City of Port Orford. Offshore rock was site of famous battle between Indians and newly landed whites in 1851. Refer to *Battle Rock, The Hero's Story.* See bibliography. Hiking, beachcombing/driftwood. View. Photography.

Humbug Mountain SP
Spectacular camping site in Brush Creek Canyon at foot of Humbug Mountain (1,750 ft. elev.). Surrounded by forest of Douglas fir, tan bark, grand fir, spruce. Trails. Spectacular view from summit. Beach accessible for beachcombing mostly driftwood. Photography.

Ophir State Safety Rest Area
Picnic tables. Site is often wind-swept. Agate beds. View. Beachcombing /floats, driftwood. Photography.

Geisel Monument SP
Forest grove. Graves of members of family massacred in Rogue Indian War on February 22, 1856. Monument. Picnic area nearby.

Otter Point State Wayside
Spectacular rocky point overlooks ocean. Beach access. Beachcombing /driftwood. Hiking. View. Photography.

Cape Sebastian SP
Crisp and windy location (sometimes heavy fog) with view to Cape Blanco (north 43 miles) and to Point St. George and St. George Reef Lighthouse (with binoculars) in California (south 50 miles).Trails. View. Photography.

Observation tower resembles lighthouse at RV park in Gold Beach. Lower view made from room in Best Western Inn of the Beachcomber.

Pistol River SP
Mouth of Pistol River at beach. Can be windy. Rolling sand dunes; beachcombing\floats, driftwood. View. Photography.

Samuel H. Boardman SP
This 11-mile narrow strip of very scenic ocean-front property with a number of off-highway parking lots. Picnics. Beach access. Beachcombing production varied due to many short beaches. Spectacular views makes this a photographer's paradise.

Harris Beach SP
Park has two areas. The camping section is east of hwy. Beach access is west of hwy with steep descent to limited parking not recommended for 5th wheels. Short sandy beach. Limited beachcombing, driftwood. Excellent views of rugged coast with many rocks. Photography.

Climbing in the rocks at Harris Beach State Park.
(Lower) An RV park at Brookings.

Private camp site facing ocean around the point on north side of Winchuck River.

Azalea SP
Park in City of Brookings on bank of Chetco River noted for varieties of azaleas. Trails. Closeup photpography of azaleas in bloom season April - June.

Winchuck State Wayside
Site on north bank of Winchuck River. View. Excellent beachcombing/driftwood. Photography. Park is undeveloped.

About the Author

James A. "Jim" Gibbs is one of those fortunate fellows to have been born and reared in the Pacific Northwest where his heritage was to enjoy refreshing ocean-borne air to breath, and salt water and ocean-going ships within sight. A native of Seattle, he graduated from Queen Anne High School that stands high atop Queen Anne Hill, where one can easily look out a classroom window and watch the marine commerce on Elliot Bay. He attended the University of Washington then joined the Coast Guard for World War II service. He was in the Coast Guard Rockaway and Pacific City Beach Patrol detachments that had been formed specifically to guard the coastline against Japanese invasion. He went to sea duty on *USCGC Nemaha* WPC-148, an Active class patrol cutter, then he did lighthouse duty on famed Tillamook Rock off the Oregon Coast. He spent four and a half years in the Coast Guard.

Jim Gibbs established the Skunk Bay Lighthouse on Puget Sound in 1965. He was employed, mostly as editor, for 20 years, of the *Marine Digest*, a Seattle maritime trade weekly.

He lived in Seattle and in Bellevue and on Maui then established Cleft of the Rock Lighthouse on the north spur of Cape Perpetua on the Oregon Coast in 1976. Cleft of the Rock is the only privately-owned working lighthouse on the Oregon Coast.

Gibbs is the author of numerous of books about lighthouses, ships and shipwrecks, as well as several magazine articles. He is the former President of the Puget Sound Maritime Historical Society, Seattle and is a deacon and lay preacher at Yachats Baptist Church.

He and his wife, Cherie, enjoy their life at Cape Perpetua. They have one grown daughter, Debbie, who, with her husband, Ray Pedrick, are near-neighbors also on the cape.

*   *   *

Bert Webber is a research photojournalist, editor and publisher. He has written and published many books on a wide variety of subjects primarily about Oregon, the Oregon Trail and World WarII.

For a list of books by Gibbs or by Webber, consult *Books in Print* which is found in most public libraries and in many book stores.

Bibliography

Baker, Lillian. *American and Japanese Relocation in World War II; Fact, Fiction & Fallacy.* Webb Research Group. 1990.

Bancroft, Hubert Howe. *History of the Northwest Coast.* Two volumes. Bancroft. 1884.

Beeson, John. (Intro. by Bert Webber) *John Beeson's Plea For the Indians; His Lone Cry in the Wilderness for Indian Rights – Oregon's First Civil-Rights Advocate.* Webb Research Group. 1994.

"Did Negro Pirate Once Terrorize Our Indians?" in *Oregon Sunday Journal* Apr. 26, 1931 p.3.

Evans, James R. *Gold Mining in Oregon.* Webb Research Group. 1994.

Franchere, Gabriel. *Adventure at Astoria 1810-1814.* Univ. Oklahoma Press. 1967.

Gibbs, James A. *Tillamook Light.* Binford and Mort. 1979.

_____. *Oregon's Seacoast Lighthouses.* Webb Research Group. 1992.

Lee, Daniel and Joseph Frost. *Ten Years in Oregon.* Private print. (N.Y.) 1844.

Nokes, J. Richard. *Columbia's River; the Voyages of Robert Gray, 1787-1793.* Wash. State Hist. Soc. 1991.

Geographic Names Information System – Oregon - (GNIS) Office of Cartographic Research, National Mapping Division, U.S. Geological Survey, Reston, Virginia. Dec. 1992. (Do not confuse with McArthur, *Oregon Geographic Names*)

Peck, William A. *The Pig War; The Journal of William A. Peck – Soldier 1858-1862 – U. S. Army Corps of Engineers.* Eds. C. B. Coulter, Bert Webber. Webb Research Group. 1993.

Smith, Dwight, James B. Norman and Pieter T. Dykman. *Historic Highway Bridges of Oregon.* Oregon Hist. Society. 1989.

Wall, Dorothy. *Yaquina Lighthouses on the Oregon Coast.* Webb Research Group. 1994.

Webber, Bert. *Battleship Oregon, Bulldog of the Navy.* Webb Research Group. 1994.

_____. *Indians Along the Oregon Trail; the Tribes of Nebraska, Wyoming, Oregon and Washington Identified.* Webb Research Group. 1992.

_____. *Silent Siege III: Japanese Attacks On North America in WWII; Ships Sunk, Air raids, Bombs Dropped, Civilians Killed.* Webb Research Group. 1992.

_____. *Wrecked Japanese Junks Adrift in the North Pacific Ocean.* YeGalleon. 1984.

Webber, Bert and Margie Webber. *Battle Rock, the Hero's Story; A True Account– Oregon Coast Indian Attack; An Oregon Documentary.* Webb Research Group. 1992.

_____. *Bayocean, The Oregon Town That Fell Into the Sea.* Webb Research Group. 1989.

_____. *I'd Rather Be Beachcombing.* Webb Research Group. 1993.

_____. *Lakeport; Ghost Town of the South Oregon Coast.* Webb Research Group. 1990.

_____. *Terrible Tilly; Tillamook Rock Lighthouse; a Biography of a Lighthouse – An Oregon Documentary.* Webb Research Group. 1992.

_____ *I'd Rather Be Beachcombing.* Webb Research Group. 1993.

Wilson, Nancy. *Dr. John Mcloughlin, Master of Fort Vancouver, Father of Oregon.* Webb Research Group. 1994.

Illustration Credits

"Pretty as a Picture" photos are shown as <u>underscored **bold**</u> type

Coquille River Lighthouse, commonly called "Bandon Lighthouse," is easily accessible from Bullards Beach State Park. It has an exciting history like the time, in 1904, when the lumber schooner *C. A. Klose* almost rammed it. The light was extinguished in 1939 but as an historic attraction, the old tower displays a small solar light.

Index

Illustrations are shown in **bold *italic*** type